ALMOST BOYS

The Psychology of Co-ed Boarding in the 1960s

ISOBEL ROSS

The opinions expressed herein are those of the author. Some names and identifying details have been changed to protect the privacy of individuals. The dialogue within the book should not be assumed to be verbatim.

This book reflects the author's present recollections of experiences over time. It may contain terms and annotations that reflect the author's opinion or that of the period in which the item was written, and may be considered inappropriate today in some circumstances.

Published by Goldcrest Books International Ltd
www.goldcrestbooks.com
publish@goldcrestbooks.com

ISBN: 978-1-913719-06-7

To the girls of Fairview House, you were (and still are) heroes.

AUTHOR'S NOTE

This narrative is based upon my diaries written between 1969 and 1971. Unfortunately, I wrote no complete diaries before then, so if I refer to events at boarding school before 1969, or from even earlier in my childhood, I am relying on memory. I hadn't read my diaries since I shoved them to the back of a cupboard at university, but they have travelled with me for almost fifty years, the pages wafer-thin, yellowed and smelling like ancient documents. At the start of the first lockdown for COVID-19 in 2020, I re-read the diaries and was immediately struck by how my thirty years' experience as an educational psychologist provided insight into what had happened to me, and around me, at boarding school. Secondly, as I read books written by other ex-boarders, or therapists who work with ex-boarders, I felt there was something missing – the stories of women like me who attended co-ed boarding. I decided to write this story, so that our voices could be heard but also to contribute to the current debate about boarding education.

Isobel Ross is not my name. Because I am using a pseudonym, I cannot identify my wonderful readers: three educational psychologists, three ex-boarders and my sister. I am so grateful for the time you all gave to reading, listening and commenting. Your contributions changed the book immeasurably and for the better. Thanks also must go to my editor, Dr Karen Ette, who has brought her eagle-eyed skills and knowledge to this manuscript. I am immensely grateful to Sarah Houldcroft at Goldcrest Books for her attention to detail, efficiency and patience in publishing my story. Particular thanks go to Piers Cross for sending me links to articles on attachment and boarding school. These were immensely useful.

CHAPTER 1

The Start

At first, there was whispering, sly looks and playground games organised without me. The bullying quickly became physical with 'accidental' knocks, thumps on the back and stones thrown as I stomped home, shoulders slouched, to a house that was too large for our village, with its gates, sweeping driveway and lawns shaded by beech trees.

The reasons for being singled out lay well beyond my control. We were incomers to the community, my mother drove her own car and worked full-time in our school as a secondary school maths teacher, educating children who hadn't passed the eleven-plus exam and couldn't move up to the high school. Worse, I spoke with a different accent and was considered 'English' by my Scottish classmates. The only surprise was that they'd waited almost a year to start bullying me.

Our playground had no adult supervision. For entertainment, revenge, or to settle grudges, fights were organised at break or lunchtime, the victim informed through a note passed in class. When my invitation to a fight landed on my desk, my stomach registered the dread, my eyes watched the clock, willing time to stop. If I stared hard enough, the hands did seem to hesitate and wobble but always jerked forward, tick-tock, betraying me. Circled by children in the playground, chanting ‘fight, fight’, my opponent would appear, supported by their cronies. I was pushed in the chest and shoved them back, my arms flailing, as if I was batting away wasps. The gathering crowd of children laughed, my opponent loomed closer and tugged my hair, and I would snatch at hers (it was always a ‘her’ because boys never fought girls) and always failed to grab her plait or bunches. Sometimes, I managed to pull off a ribbon. The crowd cheered, wanting more action. Within minutes, I was knocked to the ground and pummelled on the back.

The fights were not particularly serious, it was more about the dread and humiliation. The victor had won and it was enough to swagger in the admiration of her peers. I picked myself up, brushed down my uniform and made the lonely walk back to the cloakroom. There must have been bruising on my body but by nine years old, I was responsible for my own care, and adults never saw me naked.

Janet, a frail woman who seemed elderly, lived with us, paid to do childcare while my mother was at work. I’ve no idea how Janet filled her time through the day, but after school, she supervised an early tea for the children and watched over my brother’s bath. Once my mother returned, she disappeared into her room. One day, Janet didn’t emerge, and through her bedroom door, I caught a glimpse of a woman in bed with wild hair and desperate eyes. A sister was found, and Janet vanished. Nothing was said, except that she had died.

One Saturday, the girls who bullied me at school rang the bell of our back door. If they'd chosen to run up our long drive, I might have had a chance to warn my father, but he let them in. The girls stood cowed in our dark, high-ceilinged hall and answered my parents' questions with a politeness I had never noticed at school. In my bedroom, they started to search through my things but soon grew bored. Shrieking with laughter, they ran from the room, footsteps pounding along the corridor towards the stairs up to the attic, a place that was forbidden. I ran after them, hoping my parents might hear us but there was no reassuring bellow of authority, no heavy footsteps thundering upstairs to see what could possibly be going on, no rescue. In the attic, there was nothing but a few suitcases and a lockable door that led into eaves storage. The girls immediately saw its potential and prodded at my back until I was inside, drawing the bolt behind me. I heard whispering outside the door, then nothing.

It felt like hours until I was found. The space was dark, smelt of wood and dust, and unseen spiders would soon find me, dangling on silk threads from every beam, stroking my cheek. There was relief too. I was alone, safe, and no longer responsible for whatever desecration had followed. At last, my parents would understand what I was going through at school. Eventually, I was found, probably at lunchtime. The girls had whooped their way around the house, making an exit through the utility room into the garden where they had pulled down the soft fruit cages. My parents were furious, but it was my fault for having such badly behaved friends.

I had tried to tell my mother about the bullying, but she said I was making it up. She was a teacher, she reminded me, and teachers can always tell when a child is lying. It's possible I was one of those children who grinned when told off, or when trying to tell adults something serious, because I was often accused of lying. Some children do this because they're desperately trying to connect with the angry adult or because they haven't learned the link between facial expressions and emotions. Instead of frowning or looking sad, they smile. Alternatively, a child who feels threatened might smile in an attempt to placate the adult. If emotions haven't been modelled or encouraged by parents, the child will not be able to read facial signals or understand that it might be provocative to show a smiling face to an angry adult. Some adults persist with this defence; a recent prime minister being a good example. An inappropriate grin seems odd from an adult but in a child, it can be a red rag to a furious parent or teacher. Adults interpret the smile as defiance, as evidence of lying, or that the child is incapable of remorse.

Finding the courage to tell an adult about bullying is a huge step, risking what the bully might do if they find out. Parents and teachers sometimes fail to act because they are unsure what to do, they don't believe the child is being bullied or they think the child may be provoking other children, in other words, they deserve it. A child who isn't listened to by adults may become hopeless and defeated, with poor prospects for their later mental health. Some will rebel against their parents and teachers and develop a reputation for being hard, aggressive and disruptive, which will greatly affect their educational future. Other children may try to save themselves and take independent action, deflecting the bullies' attention, through becoming a joker and laughing at their own weaknesses before the tormentors have a chance to do so. Some bullied children will bully another vulnerable child.

This was my chosen path. I turned the attention of my persecutors towards a girl who had done nothing except be friendly towards me, persuading them that she would be an even better target. Already bored with me, they agreed, and she was ignored at Brownies, called names in class, and had her schoolwork destroyed. My shame was nothing compared to the relief at being released from my own torment.

But something exceptional happened. One day, the classroom door opened and my former friend's mother stood in front of us, welcomed into the class by our teacher. Trembling and tearful, clutching her handbag in front of her like a shield, she begged that the bullying of her daughter stop. She knew who was responsible and we were being given one chance. I felt the fear that comes before a smack, when the groin and bladder prepare for a blow. Close behind this shame, I felt the shock of love. This was what mothers do, mothers who love their child. Would my mother stand in front of us in her Dereta suit and smart court shoes, begging for the bullies to leave me alone? That would never happen. The bullying of my friend stopped overnight.

I needed another strategy to ingratiate myself. We planned a shoplifting trip to the local town and I chose to join in, taking the well-trodden route of bully victims into delinquency. Our target was Woolworths, with its 'help yourself' displays and the aisles crowded with Christmas shoppers. One by one, the other girls dropped out, leaving me with the leader. I would do the lifting and she would hide the goods. That morning, I told my parents a partial truth, that I was shopping for Christmas presents with a girl who shared my older sister's name, so they asked no questions. On the sticky, faux-leather seats of the empty bus we talked and laughed as if we were equals, and in the mirrored windows our reflections showed two young girls, chattering as if they were friends. It was fully dark by the time we arrived and Woolworth's window sparkled with tinsel, fairy lights and pastel boxes of soaps and talcum powder. We pushed through the swing doors into the sweet, sugary warmth of the store and the booming sound of Petula Clark's hit single 'Downtown'. Before the song ended, we had been caught slipping Bronnley lemon-scented soaps into our knickers and were dragged by the hoods of our raincoats into a room empty of Christmas, with only gloss-painted cream walls, a Formica-topped table and two metal chairs. The store manager questioned us, his tone heavy and bored, shaking his head when he learned how young we were. He had no choice but to call my mother, he said, but would have much preferred to ring the police. Once my mother arrived, eyes staring from a face that slipped between confusion and anger, the manager asked her to check our knickers. I had already slipped the soaps into my pocket, where they were found. My friend had hidden nothing, not in her coat, cardigan pockets or underwear. My mother asked which child had been stealing and the manager pointed at me. 'That one,' he said.

During the car journey home, my bully friend turned into a weeping, pleading, remorseful child who begged my mother not to tell her father. Children who bully are more likely to have parents who use temper to control their children, and my mother may well have met this child's father at school, through her older siblings. Whatever the reason, my mother dropped the girl at her door, choosing not to face the angry parent inside, allowing time for them to set the scene for the following day.

I didn't cry or try to explain but stayed frozen within the bizarre scene I had created. In fact, I probably smirked. My mother instructed me to pray to God for forgiveness, but since this was not long after her declaration that 'no intelligent woman' could believe in God, I ignored her. Sent to bed without food, I lay in the dark, enveloped in my chilly, slippery quilt, listening to ordinary household sounds from downstairs: the roar of the kettle, the dogs barking, my mother's voice rising as my siblings, my father and our new nanny learned of my disgrace.

Early in the morning, the telephone rang. My parents were asked to leave me at home and immediately attend a meeting with the headmaster. Hours later, they returned with my schoolbooks and my PE kit. I was the only one found in possession of stolen goods. A blameless child had been forced to support my shoplifting. I would not return to school.

The evidence of my distress was clear from my workbooks, empty of writing or numbers, every page scrawled with menacing drawings of evil faces. At last, we talked about what had happened, but it was a conversation about facts: who had bullied me, what was said or done, when were the fights? My parents pleaded with the school ... I had been the victim, it was a few days before the Christmas holidays, I had my eleven-plus exam in the spring. The headmaster's mind was made up, going back to school was out of the question. My relief was profound. I would not have to feel their eyes on me, listen to the whispering, endure the shame. But both my parents were out all day, and I couldn't be left for weeks or months with our inexperienced nanny. Now wary of employing the elderly, my mother had had a dramatic change of heart and recruited fifteen-year-old Jane to look after us. Only a few months before, Jane had failed all her 'O levels' including maths, as taught by my mother.

The Christmas holidays approached and I had to be found another school. My father telephoned the headmaster of the boarding school he had attended and there was a place for me in January. I would be welcomed into Rosehill, a small, friendly boarding house for girls, I wouldn't have to sit the entrance exam and the school didn't enter pupils for the eleven-plus. It was a miracle.

*

My memory says it was dark, but this was Scotland in January 1965, so it was probably only mid-afternoon. I had never before sat alone in the back of the car, without quarrelsome pushing from my older sister and younger brother. My hands stuck to the upholstery, steadying my balance as I swerved from side to side. My parents' low voices murmured from the front, and I watched the back of their heads, sometimes seeing their profiles, my mother's long, sharp nose, my father's short and upturned. I wore my new uniform – a blazer, square-neck blouse and pinafore – and felt a cold gap between the end of my liberty bodice and the top of my stockings. I didn't think about my siblings left behind, or the dogs, or my bedroom. I didn't think about what was to come, because I had no idea. My father told a story about the ghost of an AA motorcycle rider, who haunted this very road and I peered through the window between trails of raindrops, hoping to spot him.

We parked outside an ordinary house, lights blazing from the bay windows, even upstairs. The front door, propped ajar, cast a long, twisted rectangle of light onto the path. I stood next to my trunk in the hall, listening to adults talk above my head. It was a normal hall with a carpet, a mirror and a grandfather clock, but it smelt of food and plimsolls. A tall, thin woman with grey hair introduced me to a girl of about my age. Moira hopped onto a staircase, from the bottom step onto the next, impatient to show me upstairs. I noticed the carpet was faded and didn't stretch right across each stair but was fixed in place by brass stair rods.

My bed was flat against the wall to the left of the door, in a room with seven other beds, strewn with lumpy quilts and soft toys. This was our 'dors' or dormitory, Moira said, and you shouldn't stuff socks, pants or stockings into any old drawer of your locker or 'Ma Kent would have a fit'. I followed Moira back downstairs, keen to show my parents the bedroom, but my trunk stood alone in the hall, where they had stood. I peered at the front door, seeing shadows through the stained glass. Miss Kent bent her long neck down towards me and said they'd had to get away. It was a long drive.

From the recollections of other ex-boarders, this was normal practice. My parents may have wanted to say goodbye but they would have been firmly encouraged to leave. Fearful of the institution, they would have complied. This prevented tears or fuss from both sides, an unwelcome distraction for the matron trying to focus on settling the girls after the holidays. The natural, healthy protest expected from me would be deferred until it could be dealt with by strangers, according to tradition and protocol. Much better for the parents to sneak off.

Crying is natural when we leave someone we love, especially when we don't know if we will see the person again, which is how every separation feels to a young child. A child dropped off at boarding school may not see their parents for weeks or even months. Depending on their age, this timescale is meaningless. The parents are gone, they are alone. Most parents know that a child needs time to settle, that preparation in small steps is key and saying goodbye, no matter the immediate distress, will lay the groundwork for happier separations in future. The child learns that the parent may leave but will always come back. They can be trusted. Despite this well-established knowledge and practice, as an educational psychologist observing in early years' setting, I have often seen parents being encouraged to 'slip away' before the child has time to notice. In the face of instruction from the trained staff, the 'experts', to refuse needs a confidence most of us don't have.

Even the best prepared child, a child who has begged to go to boarding school, will cry at parting. Researchers in the field of children's boarding school experience suggest that parents who choose to send a young child away may already be uncomfortable living with a child's emotions. Because the expected and healthy tears at parting feel intolerable, the parents prefer not to witness them and are happy to hurry away.

*

Preparation for boarding school is not possible, even for a child with siblings at the school or one who has immersed themselves in boarding school stories. One day the child is at home, the following day they live in a completely unfamiliar environment with different adults, peers and routines that may seem pointless. My own preparation was frenzied and entirely practical, since the shops closed between Christmas and New Year and so much had to be bought and named. Overnight I was the centre of attention, my mother taking me alone to Edinburgh to visit the school outfitter, with lunch at Jenner's on Princes Street. On Christmas Day, I wasn't allowed to give presents in case any were stolen goods, but my grandparents and aunts excelled themselves with exciting gifts from the school list: a leather-bound writing set with Basildon Bond paper and envelopes tucked into separate compartments, a silky washbag filled with my own toothpaste, toothbrush, comb and hairbrush, a shoe cleaning kit with tiny pots of polish and miniature brushes and a sewing case that lifted apart on hinges, with tidy compartments for pristine threads, buttons and needles.

I was the centre of attention, the princess of the moment, but I didn't understand I was leaving. No one talked to me about why my primary school had finished or the place where I was going. My sister was old enough to listen in to adult conversations and overheard my parents repeat to anyone who asked that I'd 'got in with a bad crowd'. They never accepted the degree of the bullying or their own part in failing to protect me. Only one of my mother's friends said it was wrong to send a child out of the family for a misdemeanour, arguing that shoplifting was common, especially amongst children. Hurt by her criticism, my mother defended herself — they were doing their best for me, there was no choice — but for a while, she avoided her friend. I knew I wasn't going back to my old school but hadn't grasped that my taken-for-granted family would be gone and I would be on my own. Although I was ten, all I had known was this family, whatever their failings, and I could not imagine what would replace them.

Many adults who attended boarding school can still recall the first separation, a silent shock that persisted for days before the tears and loss overwhelmed them. Child development experts now believe that this shock is not 'homesickness' but bereavement, the child progressing from denial, through distress and anger, to acceptance, at a pace unique to their individual earlier experience. I didn't cry, having already learned that tears were risky in my family, and was praised for my quick 'settling in'. Initially, my abandonment felt like the noise and slow motion of being underwater. Standing alone with Miss Kent in the hall of Rosehill House, I felt nothing, hearing only a rushing sound in my ears. This was followed by weeks and months of a sensation of being separate, as if watching actors on a stage. The comfort I found in the role of observer stayed with me throughout my years at boarding school and has never left me.

Before boarding school, my attachment to my parents had already started to weaken. Our move from a farm in Northumberland to Scotland, with both parents trying to establish new careers, had meant changes in our family that went beyond domestic arrangements. My contact with them became cursory and any physical comfort or attention, already in short supply, stopped altogether. Angry about the move and resentful of being left with carers, I tried to set my mother and father tests, to see if they would remember how to parent me. Close to the eventful Christmas, when everything changed, I pulled from my satchel a model of Santa Claus I had made at school. I held it up for them to see, saying I had something to show them. When neither of them looked, I ran into the hall and ripped the Santa into small pieces, scattering it across the bottom step for my parents to step over when they went to bed. They failed these tests, as I knew they would.

My first night in the dormitory passed without sleep. The top sheet was drawn tight against my neck, with a coarse blanket on top, tucked firmly into the hard mattress.

I felt I must lie straight and not turn over. Unusual noises startled me out of snatches of sleep; girls murmuring or snorting as they moved in bed. I didn't think of home. Instead, I was preoccupied by the thought that this strange world had been here for all the time I had existed. I had stepped into a parallel universe.

In the morning, when I watched the other girls flip and tuck their sheets, the dormitory monitor showed me how to do a hospital corner. Her action was practised and efficient, but I knew I would never remember those rapid folds on my own. At the sound of a gong, Moira and Kate, the other of the three younger girls, waited beside me and we clattered down the stairs at the end of the line. The dining room had an austere fireplace, with a large ornate mirror above, and there was one long table with a white tablecloth. I sat next to Miss Henderson, the housemistress, with Kate opposite. The girls called her 'Hennie' and I'd already heard the shocking story of the girl who had dared to say: 'Yes Miss Henderson, no Miss Henderson, three bags full Miss Henderson.'

At the other end sat Miss Kent, the matron, with Moira next to her. The two oldest girls, who did not share our dormitory, sat opposite each other in the middle of the table. They looked odd in uniforms, almost too mature to be at school, and I guessed they were older than Jane. The girls bowed their heads for Miss Henderson to say a short grace. When we looked up, I noticed her staring at me, heavy eyebrows standing alert below her grey fringe. One of the senior girls poured tea. I reached for the sugar and scooped two generous spoonsful into my cup. Miss

Henderson continued to frown, her eyebrows creased into a furrow.

'Take sugar in tea if you must,' she said, 'but don't stir it. And never reach for something on the table. You must wait for it to be passed.'

The smell of porridge and eggs from the trolley made my unrested stomach queasy, but I realised that leaving food wasn't an option. A slice of bacon passed under the tablecloth ended up on my lap, and I slipped it into my pocket. One of the senior girls winked at me and as a reward, I was passed the toast, followed by the butter and marmalade. I leaned forward with my knife and scooped butter from the dish. Miss Henderson frowned at me again.

'Use the butter knife. Use the butter knife!'

*

Crowded into the cloakroom, all the girls changed into outdoor shoes, coats, scarves and gloves and I did the same, although I wasn't sure where we were going. It was still dark and would be for another hour. I followed Moira and Kate through wet, grey streets of solid, four-square Victorian houses, passing groups of older girls and boys with their arms full of books. Kate had already told me that 'Kate' was not her real name. Her given name was already taken by an older girl in Rosehill and on the day she arrived as a new boarder, she had been informed that she was now to be known as Kate, her middle name.

Boarders never used a bag or satchel, I was told by my guides, unlike day pupils or travellers. As Moira and Kate chattered, I didn't want to admit I'd expected to have lessons at the long table in the common room. We were walking to school, just like I had at home, except home had vanished. Through gates set into railings wrapped around vast lawns and mature trees, crowds of pupils in uniform surged up paths towards a solid, dark building, rows of bright windows shining through the mist like teeth. This was our school, founded by a local man who was likely to have been a slave trader, although this would not be acknowledged for several more decades.

I wanted to stand and stare but as we approached steep steps leading up to a porticoed entrance and bronze doors, we veered away and carried on up a slope behind the main building. Moira was left behind in the playground for the junior school and I followed Kate through a gap in the wall, past a row of houses, towards a bridge over a stream. A church hall, set back from the bridge, was the temporary home of primary six. Outside, a group of children shivered and blew on their hands, too cold to move.

After registration, my new teacher, a tall man who smelt of cigarettes and hair oil, called me to his desk and threw questions at me from the Scottish primary school syllabus. Satisfied with my answers, he sent me back to my desk with a page of arithmetic problems. I found them easy but checked and re-checked my answers, every shift in my chair carrying the faint whiff of bacon.

By break, I was in primary seven with Moira. My teacher walked me there himself, his gown flapping behind, questioning why I had been placed with him. I'd been in a primary seven class at my state school, he said. Had Kate made a mistake? I had no answer, other than

I'd missed a lot of work and my parents wanted me to catch up. I wasn't sure how much he knew about me, and I wasn't about to start explaining. Despite everything, I had passed his tests and there was some small pride in my parents being wrong about how much learning I had missed. Besides, I hadn't liked ending up in a church hall.

My second teacher of the morning, a heavily built man called Mr Q, nodded towards an empty desk and I took my place, looking around for Moira. Mr Q liked a quiet life. Every day began with some class teaching, then the day's tasks were chalked on the board and his newspaper and pipe were retrieved from his briefcase. Our work was marked after lunch, then we were dismissed. In between, we were free to amble around the room, chat and waste time, as long as the set work was completed. In my old classroom, left only weeks before, we sat in rows, the slower learning children at the front, the highest achieving at the back. No one moved or talked. Within twenty-four hours I had faced two seismic changes in my life, a change of home and a change of school, both functioning as polar opposites of my past experience. Rosehill House was set in the past, a living history of curtseying to adults, afternoon walks and lost property with rationing tags. My classroom was a model of relaxed, child-centred learning, undermined by the puzzling contradiction of Mr Q's simmering rage.

Mr Q didn't set any homework, perhaps because he was too idle to mark it, so during the hour and a half of supervised homework or 'prep' in the boarding house, I had nothing to do. All the girls, apart from the senior girls who had their own study, sat together in the common room around a table, heads bent over workbooks, on rough school chairs that snagged our stockings. There was nowhere else to sit in the common room, apart from two frayed armchairs in a bay window, so when we relaxed, to read or play a game, we still sat on the hard chairs around the table.

There was a house collection of tattered novels, no doubt left over from the matron's holidays, and in prep I read my way through Agatha Christie and Georgette Heyer. Peering at the older girls from under my fringe, I caught the occasional flicker of rolled eyes, the exaggerated lip movements of silent conversation, and notes passed between them. One evening, a girl in third year dropped her head onto the table and fell soundly asleep. This happened often, and when I asked Moira what was wrong, I was told she had an illness. We were all to ignore her. She did not return the following year. Another child who disappeared was a boy in my class who was ridiculed for wearing his kilt every Friday. Boy boarders wore kilts to church and to travel, so this child must be travelling, but to where? When I asked him, he said he had an appointment every Friday, naming a place I didn't know. Moira told me it was the local psychiatric hospital, a name the girls used to make fun of anyone who was different, including a man called Tom who sat on a wall outside the village sweet shop, kicking his legs and shouting.

Miss Kent, our matron, died unexpectedly in the Easter holidays. My parents told me that she had died, in much the same way I learned about Janet, giving me the few known facts. It was years since I had sat on anyone's knee, but Miss Kent liked to cuddle me while she was knitting. I wasn't too keen, because she wore a mask whenever she handled wool, and could look a bit scary. She bathed the three youngest girls every night, two of us in the bath at a time. There was nothing weird about Miss Kent's hesitant touch of our bodies, her hands discreetly protected by something called a loofah. After my bath, she wrapped me in a towel and squeezed me close to her chest, pulling the towel tight under my chin. Warmed by hot water and brief moments of Miss Kent's shy mothering, I started to sleep well, lulled by the soft voices of older girls whispering and giggling under their quilts.

The Easter holidays were my first time back with my family. I have no recollection of the transition, the packing, the car ride home, but I remember being excited and chattering to my parents about my new world, trying to explain the detail. My sister says I seemed happy, although I struggled to return to my role as a home child, instead of the boarding school child I had become. My accent had changed and I tried to put on airs and graces, even demanding a butter knife at the table. My siblings decided I was 'posh' and a bit ridiculous.

The summer term started and it seemed as if Miss Kent had never existed. For the girls in her boarding house, there was no memorial, no celebration of her life. We were not expected to grieve. The school had a dilemma. Miss Henderson was retiring and our planned merger with Fairview House, the only other girls' boarding house, meant it was impossible to find a temporary matron. Apart from mealtimes, evidence of Miss Henderson as a living being was negligible, beyond theme tunes for *Coronation Street* and *Z Cars* seeping out from under her study door but, nominally, she was in charge. Women from the village cleaned and cooked during the day, but in the evenings we were responsible for ourselves.

One afternoon, late in the summer term, Mr Q called Moira and me up to his desk and warned us that Fairview girls were brash, mouthy and too confident. He preferred Rosehill girls, he smirked, they were better mannered, more compliant. We must try hard not to become typical Fairview girls. I didn't understand what he meant at the time, but this was my first experience of a powerful myth perpetuated by boy boarders and some of the staff, that girl boarders were not vulnerable children, separated from their families but were a 'type' of girl or woman harmful to boys and men.

In Rosehill, everything changed that summer. As long as we were back before dark no one cared where we were or noticed what time we returned. Moira and I were quick to exploit this freedom, staying out as late as possible on our bikes and pedalling back to Rosehill, red-cheeked and breathless, in time for bed. Sometimes, we found healthy pursuits like tennis or athletics practice, but whenever we could find them, we hovered at the edge of a group of older boys who hung around the squash courts, the hollow thwack of squash balls and the smell of rubber and sweat the backdrop to our excitement. The squash courts were in a separate building from the sports hall, hidden in a corner of the grounds amongst bushes and trees. The boys were there to smoke but, if they noticed us at all, we became a useful distraction, playthings available to be teased or manhandled.

If being tickled or hauled onto someone's knee felt uncomfortable, the unpredictability of boys, with their deep voices and unfamiliar smell of body odour and Old Spice, was exciting and risky. The evenings were light until late but often damp with just-passed rain, so we often gathered inside the building, Moira and I watching and laughing like fan girls, until we shone briefly under the spotlight of their attention. Once, I was hung by my ankles over the balcony of the squash courts, staring at the concrete stairs below, shrieking and protesting, terrified of being dropped and horrified that my knickers were on show. Once turned upright to stand on the landing, and pulling down my skirt, I joined in with their laughter. We were learning the rules: never show emotion, never tell, pretend everything is a joke.

Inevitably, the boys powerful, adolescent sexual feelings and our need for physical affection changed our interactions. I became the favourite of one boy, and did nothing to discourage him, often sitting on his knee. Moira and I were kissed, but in ways that could still be denied. After that, the meetings stopped. We waited, hanging around the squash courts, but the boys never came back. I'm glad they saw sense. If rumours had spread, they would have faced gossip, harmful to their reputation as well as ours, or even discipline from teachers. My behaviour was unremarkable, typical of most top primary school children beginning to explore sexual boundaries with boys who seemed mature but would only have been in third year. This would have happened in my own village too, if I had remained part of the community, where most older children and adolescents gathered outside the chip shop and cafe in the evenings, joking and pairing off. Moira and I needed someone to step in, and fortunately, the boys took that step. Unknown to our parents, during the long summer evenings of that term, no one had responsibility for us apart from each other and we certainly lacked the maturity to assess any potential risk or make sensible choices.

CHAPTER 2

Who We Were

Early boarding was not encouraged. Most children at my school started at eleven, and few had attended a boarding prep school. My peers were not children from the wealthy, Scottish upper classes, who still sent their children to public schools in England. We were from middle-class families, and were being groomed to provide a steady stream of professionals to serve the populations of Edinburgh and Glasgow.

Some of our parents were farmers, or owned hotels, too overwhelmed by their seasonal workload to raise teenage children. Many others worked overseas or were in the army. Sending a child home from abroad for secondary schooling was the norm at this time, with fees paid for by the company or armed forces. A Scottish education was guaranteed and parents felt reassured that the child would thrive in an environment where a social life, sports and activities were on hand. Our parents did not expect us to join the British upper classes or to have dazzling diplomatic careers in a far-off part of the Commonwealth but did expect their money to buy access to the best Scottish universities. Wealth or titles didn't matter but being 'clever' did. If a child wasn't clever, then excelling at sport would just about do, especially if the sport was rugby.

Around the dinner table, my father had enjoyed telling tales about his own time at boarding school and made us cry by pretending that we would be sent too. No firm decision had been made, although the teasing became more serious once our cousins were boarders. This would have remained as idle chat, had the decision about boarding not been forced upon them by my expulsion from school. My family ended up in Perthshire because my parents' tenancy on one of my grandfather's farms, near Berwick-upon-Tweed, had been whipped from underneath them by his decision to sell up. They had broken their backs with hard work to make a success of the farm and their choice of an ostentatious house in a small village in Perthshire was a 'fuck off' to my grandfather. It was years before I learned they had not owned the house but rented it.

In Berwick, my mother had gently taught science to bored but pleasant girls at a convent school, with only a shared textbook and no laboratories. Teaching in Scotland, without training or enough experience, was incredibly hard. She found a job at my primary school, where kids who had failed the eleven-plus were kept back for two years of secondary education, until they could work on their father's farms or in the local sawmill. My mother tried teaching maths to this unreceptive group, until she escaped to college in Dundee to gain her Scottish teaching diploma, which allowed her to find a post at the high school.

My father lost the only role his education at agricultural college had prepared him for, and joined the ranks of the enemy, men who sold agricultural chemicals to sceptical farmers. He lacked the genial, smooth personality needed to persuade hardened, secretive men to part with their money. To cope with new careers and long hours, my mother had to employ permanent childcare, someone who would live in. Nowadays, all parents know that if you work outside the home, the time you spend with your children is when you need to be more of a parent, not less. Neither of my parents understood this, and once childcare was organised, they were off the hook. To the end of their lives, they argued that they were forced to send their children to boarding school because of me; a solution found for one had to be a solution for all. In fact, they reasoned, I owed them money. But given their hurry to hand over total care of their children to paid carers, boarding school worked well for them.

During the late 1990s and early 2000s, along with other educational psychologists, I started training on attachment theory and the impact on a child's development for relationships and learning. Before this, I knew about the importance of broken attachments but thought the theory applied to sudden, unplanned separations such as hospital admission, foster care or the death of a parent. Once it was widely understood that relationships in our first three years of life alter the development of our brains and can change the way we respond to stress, how we think, learn, make friends and choose our life partners, the implications of attachment theory for all children became clear. The link between boarding school and broken attachments was not made until early this century, but John Bowlby, the originator of attachment theory, said as early as 1972 that he would not send a dog to boarding school at age seven.

My early training sessions were held in a hotel conference room, circular tables covered with white cloths, bottled water, mints, pens and sponsored notepads at each place setting. The smell of coffee drifted in from the break-out area beyond the hall and my skin prickled at the thought of joining the others, without the chance to process what I had heard about the impact of broken attachments. I had recognised myself in the PowerPoint presentation and wanted to be left alone, staring at the swirly carpet, or scribbling with my corporate pen on the complimentary pad. Instead, I was expected to perform in the designated role of the person on my name badge and discuss these new ideas with my colleagues. This separation of the self was something my boarding school education had prepared me for, so I coped well, but before I could fully absorb the theory, or find the energy to help other professionals, I had to grieve for my own childhood. The detail mattered; I needed to talk to someone who would listen, understand and allow time to process the grief and repressed emotions of separating from my family at ten years old. I found an answer in extended psychotherapy and only recently returned to discussing with a professional counsellor the deep and long-term impact of boarding school upon the rest of my life.

Attachment theory is a template for how our earliest relationships develop and the impact these have on our emotional and social development into adulthood. About two-thirds of children are lucky enough to have a secure attachment to their parents, and this appears to be true across the world. In childhood, physical and emotional needs are met with reasonable consistency by parents and the child grows to be an adult who trusts other people and connects easily with others. The remaining third fall into three types: firstly, children with insecure attachments but who are avoidant and appear detached from the parent; secondly, those who are insecure but anxious, who may be clingy and demanding of attention – this group can be referred to as 'anxious-ambivalent'. The third group are the most troubled; children with 'disorganised' attachments. These children have often suffered early relationship trauma and struggle to develop empathy or form relationships without intensive, nurturing intervention. For the last third of my working life as an educational psychologist, this group were a priority for referral by schools, since they are at greater risk of poor life outcomes than other children.

Children with an insecure-avoidant or insecure-anxious attachment profile rarely come to the attention of mental health professionals since their response is organised and consistent. They may achieve in school and in their careers, but without self-reflection and taking positive steps to change, many struggle with relationships throughout their lives.

By school age, children who have an anxious-avoidant attachment profile can be astute at reading another person's emotional state while avoiding emotion and intimacy. These children and adolescents can seem independent or indifferent but have a deep-seated anxiety about rejection or showing vulnerability. They value control and try to keep relationships tightly managed. Short-lived outbursts of anger are common in this group.

Children with an anxious-ambivalent attachment profile are equally anxious but in school are often the centre of dramas with their peers. These children show off or act as the 'class clown' and demand their teachers' time and attention. Adolescents with an ambivalent profile desperately want relationships but are sensitive to criticism and exaggerate the risk of being let down or excluded by their friends. Their need for emotional reassurance is constant but they rarely notice this need in others or reciprocate.

An avoidant relationship style seems to be common amongst adults who boarded at traditional British prep and public schools. An avoidant personality fits well into the social norms of the British ruling class and is both shaped and encouraged by the public school. Since a child's relationship characteristics are formed by their earliest experience, it is unlikely that boarding schools are entirely responsible for this avoidant profile, even for children who are sent to boarding prep schools from six or seven years of age. Parents who are comfortable sending very young children away from home, to be cared for by others, may well be those who are already indifferent to their child's emotional needs. Even in the child's first few years, crucial for the development of later relationship capacity and flexibility, they have already neglected to provide good enough parenting.

Avoidant parents are often unavailable, physically and emotionally, but if they do try to be involved with their child, they can be controlling and disregard the child's wants, hopes and feelings. This description neatly captures the caring style of most adults in most boarding schools, where children are kept busy and ruled by gongs and bells, indifferent to their personal needs.

If we accept that children bring their attachment style with them to early boarding, rather than the public school being the source of the attachment profile, the child with an existing avoidant response is more likely to fit in. They will already show a narrow range of emotion, make light of everything and never make a fuss. They will be team players and perform well in the classroom without making any obvious effort or building a relationship with their teacher.

Boarding pupils at my school arrived with a range of attachment styles typical of any group starting out at a new school. My school friends were not battle-hardened prep school survivors but were ordinary children who had lived at home until the day before we were left in our dormitories. Home life for children has a monotonous and barely noticed continuity: street, school, city, friends, activities and, of course, parents, whatever their idiosyncrasies and limitations. Suddenly removing this continuity will feel shocking. Home can no longer be taken for granted, it becomes a vivid but unreal place as the child struggles to understand new routines, meets a peer group they must live with for twenty-four hours a day, and faces the loss of their unique status as a child within a family. Living within a group, the child's personality quirks no longer matter; they are constantly visible and have no choice over companions. To fit in, they may adapt by developing a boarding school self and a home self, neither of which feel real or true.

My attachment profile at school entry was characteristic of an anxious-ambivalent child, the relationship style least conducive to thriving in a traditional prep or public-school environment, where expressions of emotion are discouraged. For those of us without the bedrock of a secure attachment, or the more culturally acceptable anxious-avoidant attachment style, the social environment of boarding school was like having to make a dress without a pattern, every single day. In time, I appeared to thrive, but the effort to fit in required constant masking of my insecurity and fears. Always, there was a grumbling sense that something wasn't quite right and feelings of exhaustion from continually monitoring relationships. Anxiety was my constant escort and at times I felt overwhelmed by stress, showing as physical symptoms such as heart palpitations. As early as primary seven, when I had only been boarding for a term, I wrote to my parents with worries about my heart and its irregular beats. My family's history of heart disease was well known to me and I thought I was about to die. Despite appearances, I hadn't settled well; in fact my distress was showing itself as panic. This surprising news about my heart passed censorship and when they read it, made my parents laugh.

Because of my divided self I refused to accept any invitations to stay with Fairview girls in the holidays, much to my mother's embarrassment. I did not want to reveal the holiday, family child to my boarding friends and the worry of surviving within the complex rules of another family felt overwhelming. What if my friend was as different as I felt myself to be, without the props of school and the boarding house? The termly separation from home, returning to school after each holiday, was more than enough.

In my first year in Fairview, once my family had moved to live in Fife, I was invited to the cinema by a school friend who lived in a nearby town. I couldn't think of a good enough reason not to go. A refusal risked disappointing my parents who couldn't hide their delight that I might, at last, make a local friend, instead of hanging about at home, staring out of the window or teasing the dog. A refusal also risked making an enemy of Eloise, who could not be avoided at school. Although Eloise was in my form, she may well have been almost two years older than me.

When I was dropped off by my father, he stared at Eloise, who was inches taller, and wore a shorter-than-short miniskirt, long boots and a scarf draped around the neck of her thigh-skimming polo neck. My home self was a child whose parents hadn't yet grasped that clothes mattered, whereas at school, such differences could be hidden by uniform. I was dressed in my school blazer instead of a jacket, baggy corduroy jeans and a thin, misshapen top, the colour of caramel custard. Eloise raised her eyebrows but said nothing. Our evening together passed, helped by having to face forward in front of a screen. We were polite but had little to say to each other. Back at school, Eloise didn't use our uncomfortable evening as an excuse to laugh at me, as I had feared. Her only comment was that her mother had been surprised by how much younger I was.

*

No matter how securely attached to their parents, all children will feel homesick when they arrive at boarding school and must grieve according to their pre-existing attachment style. Some therapists argue that securely attached children may require the most support after separation as the betrayal will be felt so deeply. However, a securely attached child is more likely to be able to ask for and receive help from others, including their parents, and may be more open at home about their anger and distress. The natural grieving process at separation was not helped by a practice adopted by most boarding schools in the 1960s. New children were encouraged to 'settle in', which meant that we did not see our parents for three months, although we were allowed letters. If a child cried, missing their parents, we were asked to leave them alone and not comfort them; our first lesson in dampening down emotions. We were happy to comply, none of us wanting to face a raw reminder of our own recent abandonment. This emotional quarantine was a deliberate, if unconscious, attempt to weaken a child's attachment to their family, based on methods honed over centuries. The goal was to diminish the child's attachment needs and encourage identification with the school ethos and culture, allowing new attachments to be made within the peer group.

If I did not start boarding with a secure attachment profile, was it possible for those who did to lose this and take on the avoidant profile so valued in this type of school? Since society firmly believes that, with the right help and support, a child's attachment profile can change for the better, from a disorganised or insecure profile to a secure profile, we must accept that it might work the other way, particularly if the child boards from an early age and has little contact with home. The child may try to adopt the preferred avoidant profile, once they learn that emotions are not valued or trusted in their new environment. While my peers did not swell the ranks of government in later life, we may have brought our avoidant relationship style and lack of empathy into our careers as doctors, teachers, or lawyers, where understanding and compassion are crucial to decisions made at work.

One of the most puzzling questions about boarding school education is the common practice of parents to send their children to a school where they were unhappy themselves. Attachment theory helps us to understand this. For a few years and at considerable expense, the parents can again try to earn the yearned-for attention of teachers, even those who may have ignored or even harmed them. They can freely walk the hallowed halls and playing fields of an institution where they had perhaps made their only lifelong attachments with close friends and the school itself. I recently visited my former school and, standing outside my father's boarding house, with its blank windows, hunched against a background of brown hills, hearing the cries of scavenging seagulls, I felt his loneliness.

At eight years old, he had been separated from his beloved mother and would not see her again for four years. Born and raised in India, everything about Scotland was unfamiliar to him, including the cold and the awful food, yet it was to this school he had turned for advice, not his parents, when faced with a crisis about my schooling. Through my own years as a pupil, I was embarrassed by my father whenever he spoke to teachers and other former pupils, sharing jokes about members of staff from his time, recalling a caning for refusing to eat the food, or stories about spending his school holidays in a house in Fife with other boarders who couldn't go home. My father had trouble belonging, with fitting in anywhere, but in those few years when his children were boarders, he was able to come home.

CHAPTER 3

The Boarding House

There were five boarding houses for boys. After we merged with Fairview, only one girls' house remained. Most female pupils were day girls and relationships between us were not always cordial. The day girls called us 'tarts who hang around the boys' houses', a common view based entirely upon our status as girls educated away from our families and in a minority within the boarding community. Of course we hung around with the boy boarders, what else were we to do? The family is where a child belongs and the day girls were a constant reminder that our mothers and fathers were no longer available to us. If the day girls thought we were privileged, I resented their privilege, the aura they carried of being cherished and protected.

Boarders were not encouraged to mix with day pupils and this rule was closely followed until the late 1960s. In my junior year, I made friends with a girl called Rosie, and her mother wrote to Miss Henderson asking if I could come to tea after school. When this was refused, Rosie avoided me, her expression closed and guarded and we stopped being friends. There were obvious safeguarding reasons, but over-vigilance in enforcing this rule narrowed our social opportunities. It would have benefitted us to make friends with day girls and meeting their mothers may have helped us adjust to our separation from our own families. It is hard to imagine our parents would have objected, as long as consent had been sought and given.

In my first winter living in Fairview, I wouldn't hurry back to the boarding house after school. Instead, I stayed behind in the dusk, on the school steps, watching the day girls amble towards their lamp-lit homes, chattering in groups. I felt an aching hunger for a place that might feel homely. Even without a parent actually present, the parents' homemaking would create a continuity of care for these girls. There would be a gas or electric fire, a television, a tin of biscuits, coats and shoes in the hall. During term time, I struggled to remember my home, even though my older sister was now a boarder. It seemed to exist behind an opaque wall, a place that never truly came into focus. School was real and vivid, each moment lived in the present but couldn't be talked about at home. My parents' interest was limited and explanations of the cultural minutiae felt too lengthy and complicated. Unsure and lacking confidence about their decision to send us away, once we were at home it was clear they did not want to hear about our lives at school, embedding and reinforcing the gap between our home selves and our school personalities.

Many boarders gradually become outsiders within their home community, but my separation had been sudden and total. The village was no longer a place of safety and any friendships were over. In the woodland below our house, there were daffodils at Easter and I felt brave enough to scuff amongst piles of fallen leaves, moving aimlessly towards the wrought-iron gate that set our garden apart from the road. Someone called out my name and I froze. Other voices pleaded, wheedling and encouraging, inviting me out to play. It wasn't chance; they'd been expecting me, waiting for me and would be there every single day of the holidays. I turned and ran, afraid of them climbing over the gate and chasing me. I became a prisoner, unwilling to go beyond the house in case I met my former tormentors. Not even the garden was safe.

*

At school we were free to roam, annoying the locals by dominating the streets of the small town where we lived, or exploring the hills and glens that formed a backdrop to our community. Walking, or the outdoors generally, is of limited interest to children and adolescents, particularly in winter. Contrary to the promises of the school brochure, if we didn't play for a sports team, there was nothing to do. Even choir practice or individual music lessons happened only once a week. We were expected to trudge back to Fairview after school and remain in our common room until tea, without a hot drink or anything to eat. This particular deprivation seems so unnecessary, since a drink and snack, perhaps only bread and jam, would have contributed greatly to our well-being. There are now national standards for boarding schools and access to food and drink outside set meals is regarded as essential.

After tea there was prep, supper and bed. The more studious girls would start their homework straight after school but the rest of us squeezed onto one storage heater and passed around old copies of *Jackie* or *Mirabelle*. Weekends were the worst for boredom, particularly on wet, cold winter days. On Friday night we had to attend dance classes with the boy boarders, on Saturday night there was an outdated film in the school hall and on Sunday morning we went to church. On Sundays, we were expected to write to our parents after breakfast, sitting together around the table in our form room, struggling with fountain pens with ink barrels and bottles of Quink, envying those who had cartridge pens. We couldn't tell the truth about the food, the cold, or the matron's latest diatribe, because the letters were left unsealed. Pleas to be rescued from bullying, our sadness at our separation from home, any cry for help, would never have been written. Even if our letters hadn't been read by the housemistress or matron, we would not have been able to form the thoughts, never mind find the words. Because we didn't know what to say, any girl who had written her ten lines quickly would pass it around for the rest to copy. Other than this highlight, there was an entire day to fill, without enough warmth or anywhere comfortable to sit. We were not allowed to visit our dormitories except at bedtime, so the pleasure most teenagers take in lounging on their bed was unknown to us.

It is hard to understand what our parents thought they were paying for. Did they believe that depriving their daughters of ordinary home comforts was good for us, somehow character-forming, or did they not think about us enough to check on our actual living conditions or how we spent our time?

Other than sports fixtures, the school laid on no weekend activities and even the art rooms, library and music rooms were closed. We started to experiment with seances and Ouija boards, kneeling in a circle around a girl prostrate on a blanket, chanting. We were never successful in raising evil spirits – not even the dead chose to spend their time with us. When Marie marched out of one of our seances, declaring it to be 'unhealthy', she was probably right. The repetitive chanting and rhythmic movement did produce an altered state of consciousness, which helped to pass the time.

In 1969, the older girls were saved from hours of vacuous boredom when a social club for seniors opened. The club was housed in a former school building, right next to the school grounds, the brainchild of a newly qualified teacher young enough to recall his own teenage years in the wastleland of the 1950s. There was a kitchen, with a kettle, tea and coffee, a large hall with table tennis and board games, where we danced to records on Saturday nights, and a smaller, quiet room, likely to have been the former staffroom. Prefects supervised the club in the afternoons, a duty which can't have been popular. I know there was a rota because I recorded in my diary that someone had defaced it. I was volunteered for a club subcommittee for Alteration and Redecoration, which met once. Our grandiose and unbudgeted plans were turned down by school management and there is no further reference to meetings in my diary. We took the club for granted, but it was a miracle, a safe place to meet away from the streets, cafes and smokers' haunts, rescuing us from our desolate weekends.

For the younger girls, there was nothing. Crafts and games were only available if a boarder brought them from home and there wasn't a house library. Empty hours and sterile rooms made it even harder for new girls to adjust to living away from the comfort of home. Most young boarders clung to the order of the boarding house day, with gongs for mealtimes, the silence of prep and the strict sequence of bedtimes, finding some comfort in routine. The more resilient crushed their feelings with self-imposed order, through hobbies such as stamp collecting, jigsaws or scrap albums. Consistent, repetitive routines are the bedrock of infant care and the rhythm of these creates a secure base for the baby's developing relationship with their parents. The self-imposed tasks of younger boarding pupils were the child's attempt to create new, soothing routines, to help them fill the empty hours without their parents.

Former boarders still find comfort in 'busyness' and order, using this to avoid conflict in relationships and suppress troublesome emotions. The ex-boarder is a list-maker, a volunteer, a committee member, a daily gym user; anything to fill the void. I found solace in taking photographs on my box Brownie and cataloguing these in an album. I still have these out-of-focus pictures, with neat inscriptions underneath, as if trying to record a lost tribe or civilisation. I read any book I could, hiding my face in the head-down, eyes-averted position of a reader, finding yet another new world where I could lose myself. The books lying around the boarding house were not always suitable for an imaginative, anxious child. Reading Dennis Wheatley at eleven years old flooded my mind with grim images, even more than those fears fuelled by the creaks and groans of an old house settling for the night.

⁂

The women who cared for us were single, apart from those drafted in from the village to cook and clean, who were the only 'Mrs' we met. Even at school, the female teachers were proudly 'Miss', apart from the domestic science teacher. The housemistress and the matron had separate sitting rooms in Fairview leading off from the entrance hall, the public face of the house, with carpets, a wide sweeping staircase, and a rosewood table with fresh flowers. There was a telephone cubicle for the girls to use, with permission, and when we whispered to our parents, sitting on a telephone chair amongst coats and cleaning fluids, we strained to catch the moment when the housemistress or matron would turn down the volume of their televisions to hear our conversation.

The housemistress for Fairview taught in the school and was deputy head, with overall responsibility for girls. She was reputed to have been a former beauty. I was reluctant to believe this until I complained about her to a long-serving English teacher. His gaze drifted to a distant point beyond the window and he described the day she had first walked into the staffroom. She was the most beautiful woman in the world, he'd said. The housemistress was a good teacher but out of her depth in a boarding house, looking after girls. Unlike Saggy, the matron, she was in full control of her emotions and her dislike oozed through lips twisted with distain and sarcasm. We called her AyCee, a corruption of the initials of her first and last name.

Both the housemistress and Saggy wore the standard uniform of Scottish professional women: tweed skirt ending mid-calf, a blouse with a bow at the neck, a grey or brown cardigan over the shoulders, thick, brown tights and flat shoes with crepe soles. AyCee was statuesque, encased in solid foundation garments, but Saggy was the opposite and would have benefitted from a professional bra fitting. She had round, staring eyes and a rictus grin, even when she was in full meltdown, which made her appearance even more terrifying.

One afternoon after lunch, in my second year, I tried to make my friends laugh by performing a silly dance, unaware that one of the women who worked in the kitchen was staring at me through an open hatch. The laughter grew because of the expression on her face, not my dancing, and I gradually became aware that my clowning around couldn't be that funny. I spun around to face her, grinning. She scowled back and said, 'The only reason you're here is because your parents don't love you.'

Children who are unloved, or who believe they are unloved, feel a deep sense of shame, since the love of parents, particularly the love of a mother, is a core belief at the heart of our society. To be unloved by parents is so beyond the norm, a child will blame themselves for their rejection, believing they must be worthless. At the very moment of this woman's harsh words, said without thought and no doubt soon forgotten, I felt something inside me fall away. Here was more evidence that I was unlovable, even by my parents. Within minutes, I pretended to recover, laughing and clowning all over again in a desperate attempt to show everyone that it didn't matter at all. Her words were funny and anyway, I didn't care.

All adults are important in an education setting, since we can never know which passing, thoughtless comment can hit a child like a missile. When our team of psychologists was commissioned to train a full school staff on emotional well-being, we tried to include lunchtime staff, although this was not always possible. The lunchtime supervisors were a joy to work with, openly sceptical about our theories and honest in their personal disclosures. The first session often involved tears and anger about chances missed, their unfair treatment at school and parents who hadn't valued education for girls.

*

Any 'old girl' from the 1930s visiting Fairview in the 1960s would have felt at home. Here were the same rooms, with wooden lockers, utility tables and chairs, cracked linoleum, brittle, see-through toilet paper, inedible food, chilblains and tepid baths. The house photographs, which lined the walls, showed rows of girls unchanged in dress or hairstyles over decades. What these old girls would not have recognised was the background hum from a changing world.

On a Saturday morning, we cleaned our uniforms to *Junior Choice* with Ed 'Stewpot' Stewart, using a clothes brush (regulation and named) and soapy water to remove any stains, remembering to brush fluff from inside the pockets, prior to inspection by Saggy. We joined in with the songs, drowning out Saggy yelling at anyone who had 'woe betide' left behind a stain on her skirt. At night, under the covers, we tuned in to the distant crackle of Radio Luxembourg.

Society's expectations of girls were the same as ever; if a boy touched you, it was your fault, if you allowed sex before marriage, you were damaged goods, but young people like us were starting to enjoy challenging the old order. By the late 1960s our hemlines rose, and we now bought our underwear from Woolworths, rather than the school outfitters, refusing to wear the double layer of heavy-duty navy knickers on top of more ordinary pants. This meant regular knicker inspections, where we lined up and raised our skirts to be checked by Saggy. We wore our hair long and our fringes even longer, and although we left the house wearing one of the approved hairstyles, it wasn't long before we freed our hair from restraining bands and grips, until we were spotted by a prefect and given lines. Make-up was forbidden, but we smeared our cheeks with Pan Stick to cover our spots and, in the school toilets, clumped our lashes together with thick mascara.

Life within Fairview became a constant battle against petty rules. We treated debit points as a joke, trying to earn as many as possible, but management fought back with the cruel punishment of 'gating' – forcing a girl to isolate in the boarding house all weekend, or longer, for the most minor offence, such as leaving out a mug. Saggy's method was to get a girl on her own to humiliate and shame her victim through one of her uncontrolled rages. I was protected by her sly ambition to gain the respect of my mother, who was now deputy head of a large, co-ed school, but she did catch me alone once, with an untidy bed. Being screamed at by Saggy, isolated in the dormitory, left me silent and shaken for the rest of the day. But for Annie, it wasn't a solitary incident, the screaming happened to her every day. We overheard that she stank, her pants were filthy, her uniform was a disgrace, she needed to brush her hair, she looked like a tart ... in fact, she was a tart. Since she would not change, refused to benefit from advice, she deserved her humiliation. Annie's parents, like ours, had chosen to send her to this school, she was privileged to be there, so we believed her cruel treatment must be necessary, even though we hated Saggy. If we were present during Annie's daily evisceration, as we often were, we lowered our heads and thought of something else. Annie was older than us but everyone knew she was bullied by the girls in her form. It is certain, from everything that psychologists and educators know about bullying, that she became a target because adults' behaviour made her vulnerable. Their bullying promoted and condoned the same treatment from her peers.

*

The boarding house year had its own rituals and routines. At Halloween, we found a bag of sweets next to our plates at teatime, and sometimes played half-hearted games like bobbing for apples. On bonfire night, were allowed out after tea to the sports field. There was no bonfire, but boarders were free to roam, letting off fireworks if they could afford to buy any. It was exciting to be out after dark on a weeknight, to smell the gunpowder as we approached the field, but we stayed in a tight group, mingling with crowds of children waving sparklers, the clouds and stars in the night sky masked by drifting smoke. There were adults at the edge of the field, but supervision was minimal. The atmosphere felt threatening, not fun. After panicking teachers helped a screaming boy to drag a boot from his leg, because someone had dropped a lit banger down the top of his wellington, the girls decided not to stay.

At Christmas, the common rooms were decorated with faded paper chains, but a Christmas tree never graced our splendid hall, although it was the perfect setting. There was a special tea followed by a boarding house party where each dormitory put on a play. This was the era of Monty Python, and everyone tried to be clever with ironic and pointless skits. One year, we recreated *Snow White and the Seven Dwarves*. The intended joke was that Snow White would be followed by a never-ending stream of dwarves, but we failed to check whether our plan would work. Snow White's job was to play the music tape and call the dwarves one by one. Our costumes were so derisory, it was unlikely anyone in the audience would have guessed who we were without us being named. The dwarves strutted past the audience one by one, waving and mimicking the jaunty stroll of a Disney dwarf. The moment each dwarf was through the door, she ran up the back stairs, through the attic dormitories and back down the front stairs, to re-join the procession. It wasn't easy to keep up, so there were long, puzzling episodes of music without any dwarves. No one laughed and after several rounds, Snow White calling out into an empty space and the dwarves exhausted and red-faced, the management told us to stop. During our cast debrief, we decided that one of the many problems with Fairview was the absence of a sense of humour. Apart from us, of course.

Birthdays were another ritual. There was no birthday card or gift from the house, but we enjoyed buying cheap bath salts or a packet of sweets for each other, always carefully wrapped and piled next to the girl's breakfast place. Parents were required to provide a cake for the whole house but some girls begged their parents to forget. It was an ordeal to stand and listen to the false sincerity of the staff singing 'Happy Birthday' knowing that the truce would last only until the end of the meal. The birthday girl was expected to cut their cake into fifty even pieces, under the critical gaze of Saggy and sighs from the housemistress. The ordeal of slicing and passing cake stretched out into a timeless void of restless girls. My mother always sent a cake, delivered in good time from a reputable baker in St Andrews, but I didn't appreciate her efforts. Instead of the passable-but-sickly cakes ordered by most parents from a local baker and delivered straight to the boarding house, I had to pick up my cake from the post office. One horrible year, I forgot about half-day closing. Despite banging on the barred post office door, I couldn't pick up my birthday cake. When the absence of cake was discovered, it was my fault, and I was berated for my thoughtless attitude towards others. I was privileged to receive a cake at all, one of the highest quality, and the humiliation was soon forgotten, but this is an example of the small, daily cruelties endured by children who are left in the care of adults employed to look after them. Not even a 1960s parent would have expected a teenager to know about half-day closing, never mind plan for it. The organisation was relying on my cake to supplement the boarders' tea, and I was to blame not only for the inconvenience of having to find more cake in the pantry, but also messing-up the week's housekeeping. I wrote to my mother telling her how much everyone had enjoyed her cake but chose not to mention my oversight.

Group care is essential for some children – those who have been removed from their families due to neglect, sexual or emotional abuse or domestic violence – if a foster family cannot be found. While the best of group care is nurturing and life-enhancing, it cannot replace a family. Adults paid to care for children, inevitably only present for their shift, may care deeply about their charges but there is something missing. Some writers have called the missing element love, but paid carers can love the children they look after. From my reading and experience of child development, I propose that the missing element is a parent's capacity to know the child's mind, to treat the child as someone with thoughts and feelings and to use this insight to help the child understand their own mind and those of others. In the birthday cake scenario, an adult who was able to 'hold me in mind' would have thought about me, remembered half-day closing and reminded me, or might even have collected the cake themselves. Staff who work in group care, or with the most distressed young people in schools, are trained to hold a child in mind but parents do this without thinking. Parents are not perfect, will make mistakes, forget important things, or overlook what matters to the child, but as long as they are reasonably consistent with holding their child in mind, their child will thrive.

Within homes where boarding is the cultural norm, the parents do not recognise that they have all the skills and qualities required to raise their own children and are free to make a different choice. Despite having every resource available, such parents still send children as young as six or seven years old away to boarding school, paradoxically opting for a solution that wider society reserves for the most troubled families. The selling point for parents, I am told, is that the child will become resilient and learn to 'stand on their own two feet', something we all achieve in good time and without any additional cost.

CHAPTER 4

Unregulated Adults

My first encounter with a teacher who screamed was in my second year of infant's school. Miss B was a small woman with greying hair. When I describe her as screaming, I mean she was out of control; her face red, spit gathering at the corner of her mouth and shaking with rage. Miss B liked to discipline us by using a ruler on our thighs and this was particularly frightening if she hit us during one of her meltdowns. She smelt musty, from mothballs or clothes hung in a damp wardrobe. I noticed this because I was one of the children who had to stand close enough for her to reach my legs.

I was hit once a week at the same time. Every Friday morning, we had a mental arithmetic test, which I always failed. Although I was a typically developing child, I had a problem processing information that was presented orally, without visual backup, so mental arithmetic was one area where I could not be successful. Since I failed to meet the pass mark, I was smacked on the upper thigh with a ruler after every test. There was no improvement in my learning and Miss B's frustration grew. She became even more furious, week after week, spitting with anger into my face as she wielded her ruler.

We are used to young children showing limited emotional regulation; it is regarded as part of childhood, a developmental phase that resolves itself in time, although for some children the process may be slow. Unregulated adults are a different matter, and inexplicable rages would now be considered unacceptable behaviour from an adult in charge of children. What had gone wrong for Miss B? Neglect or indifference in our earliest years can mean a child remains stuck with a developmentally young way of expressing emotions. When a loving parent provides consistent care, soothes and explains troubled emotions until the child is able to regulate themselves, this is called 'containment'. As a young child, Miss B is likely to have experienced neglect, a lack of containment and the possibility of threat, which may not necessarily have been actual threat but fear caused by a parent who was present but emotionally absent. Although Miss B was able to cope in most aspects of her daily life, high stress levels caused her to become unstable and unpredictable. For the children in her care, school was no longer a secure base. We became cautious, less playful and more anxious around her. Watchful of her mood and afraid of making a mistake, Miss B became even more frustrated with us because we weren't listening properly, we didn't remember instructions and we couldn't grasp new learning.

I started to be sick in class, vomiting just before I was hit, and Miss B arranged for the caretaker to stand nearby with his mop and bucket. At home I developed what is now called Emotionally Based School Anxiety (EBSA), crying at bedtime, with headaches and stomach-ache in the morning. Of course, in the early 1960s we were not allowed to have a problem that was emotionally based, or to refuse school. The cycle of test-vomit-bucket only ended when Miss B casually asked if my mother was sending me to school after an unsuitable breakfast. The gulf between parents and school in the 1960s was vast. Families were happy to leave teachers alone and vice versa, but when I passed on Miss B's comment about my mother's breakfasts, her rage was impressive and all the better for not being directed at me. My parents rarely went into school on my behalf but my mother had to defend her breakfasts. The weekly tests didn't stop but smacking with a ruler did, and I was no longer sick.

Most of us were smacked by our parents in the 1960s and many remember the sensation. There was the pain of the hit itself but also another feeling, a rush of sensation to the groin, often resulting in a small leakage of urine. Being hit by our parents was bad enough but corporal punishment from a strange adult, in the unfamiliar setting of school, gave rise to fear, shame and terror about the loss of bodily fluids, in my case vomit. Despite friendly, relaxed maths lessons over many years, whenever emotion entered the picture, my carefully practised skills and ability to think clearly would vanish. In maths exams I panicked, flooded with anxiety, and yes ... wet myself.

It is puzzling that I didn't tell my parents about Miss B. Only the year before I had reported a taxi driver for a brief episode of sexual abuse. Because we lived on a farm, a group of us were picked up in a taxi. As the youngest, I was crushed into the bench seat at the front, next to the driver. One day he started searching my clothes, checking that I had my dinner money, but within seconds his hand was into my underwear, then quickly back onto the steering wheel. It was so fast, I wasn't entirely sure what had happened, but I did tell my mother and we never had that driver again. The difference is that Miss B was a teacher and carried with her the respect and authority of her role. Young children expect teachers to be right, so if I had to be punished for failing mental arithmetic tests, I must deserve it. If I told my parents, they might be angry too.

In primary seven, at boarding school, Mr Q was slow to move or show any emotional reaction, unless driven to rage by a day girl called Lesley. Lesley openly flirted with our awkward, prepubescent boys, causing them to squirm and redden with embarrassment. She also provoked Mr Q with a steady drip of critical wit and sarcasm. In a split second, he would travel across the room with unimagined reserves of speed, before throwing Lesley into the corridor with sudden and violent force, where she stayed until the next break. Although I felt uncomfortable during his rages, I wasn't scared, because his outbursts had a degree of predictability. We watched them build, as did Lesley. It seemed to us, her peer group, that this was what she wanted.

For children who already have an insecure attachment profile, such reactive teacher behaviour can further embed the uncertainties of their early parenting and there is reassurance to be found in this. Children like Lesley are highly anxious and seek comfort by being able to predict and control adult behaviour, even if the adult's behaviour is unreasonable, or even harmful towards them. Recognising that the child's family drama is being re-enacted in the classroom, an experienced teacher will intervene with warmth and relationship-based strategies to break the cycle.

Many of our teachers lost their temper, but it was usually controlled and faked. If another teacher knocked on the classroom door and entered, they would be met by a smiling, calm colleague, capable of holding a sensible conversation. Once the door closed behind the visitor, the shouting would begin again. But a small group of male staff, who had been young teachers at the school before the Second World War, were rumoured to have come back horribly changed. These days we would be concerned about their unpredictable rages, they would be offered help or disciplined, possibly both. These teachers were terrifying because there was no provocation, no reason for the outburst, and behind the eyes, no self-control. I was frightened by these rages, but the girls were not given the belt or Scottish 'tawse' – a leather strap with a split, designed to increase pain. When one of these traumatised teachers removed all the boys from the classroom and belted them in the corridor with the tawse, there was no obvious trigger or cause, just a red mist that demanded aggression. Some traumatised children can only find relief from habitual anxiety and hypervigilance through the brief period of calm that follows an outburst. This may also may have been true of our explosive teachers. For the boys, being punished with the tawse was bad enough from a teacher who was in full control of their emotions, but from a teacher who had lost control, it must have been terrifying.

Within our brains, the amygdala is responsible for triggering the survival response of fight or flight, often seen as either an intense anger or fear reaction. During an amygdala meltdown, anger, fear, or both overwhelm our ability to think or even recall what we might have said or done. This explains why adults who flip into intense bouts of anger or fear may deny it or minimise the degree of their reaction. A childhood with enough parental containment promotes the development of the frontal cortex, creating complex connections that allow for greater calm and reasoned actions, instead of being overwhelmed by rage or fear.

In my work, such outbursts were common reasons for referral to an educational psychologist, the best example being a fifteen-year-old boy who denied he had punched a hole in a corridor wall, despite the grazes on his knuckles, until he saw the CCTV film. In the truth-based culture of schools, denial can result in a worse outcome for the student since they are thought to be lying, or worse, incapable of showing remorse. At my boarding school, denial would have been regarded as 'dumb insolence' and if the accused was a boy, he would have been belted.

Amongst the group of teachers who were believed to have suffered emotional harm during the war was a small man we called Lucky. It was impossible to learn in Lucky's classes, because of fear and the anticipation of fear. In preparation for this book, a boarding school friend said she had never before witnessed a temper like Lucky's. He made frequent use of the tawse, but it was his pathological dislike of wasps that drove him into an amygdala meltdown. The incident would build slowly, with Lucky pausing in his teaching or writing on the blackboard, his head tilted to one side, to better hear the irritating drone. This was our warning. Typically, the wasp would be passing the time of day by trying to escape through a window pane. Our eyes scanned the room and if we found the wasp, we tried to help it escape. We would be shouted at for being out of our seats, but at least a terrifying rage had been averted. If the buzzing continued, as it almost always did, exaggerated by the deep silence that fell over the pupils, Lucky would stalk the rows of desks trying to spot the intruder, rolling up a newspaper in his hands as he prowled. Once spotted, Lucky swiped at the insect with wild sweeping motions, as if serving at tennis. Pupils in the window seats ducked, or dropped out of their seats to the floor, just before their desk and chair toppled over. The wasp invariably escaped into the centre of the room and sought refuge amongst the strip lights. Climbing onto a desk and leaping from desktop to desktop, Lucky aimed ineffective blows at the light fixtures, which he could not reach. Then he paused, as if in a trance, and scanned the room, climbing down from the desk and straightening the chairs. Any boy caught laughing was taken into the corridor for the belt and girls were given one hundred lines to complete overnight. Afterwards, Lucky turned to the blackboard and carried on writing, even if the wasp decided to make its heavy way back to the window and carry on with its needless droning and knocking against the panes.

I was confused, never quite sure whether Lucky was truly out of control or whether he was trying to be funny, except it wasn't fair or funny to punish us so severely. In the end, I decided that these episodes were simply another example of the mad world I had joined and stored them away as stories to amuse others.

Lucky had a heart attack one afternoon, falling right where he stood, enjoying an after-school smoke. The school emptied for the day and I was one of the pupils who walked past him, lying prone on the stone slabs. In the few minutes I was part of this scene, before I walked away, not a single pupil stopped or knelt to check on him. Thankfully, Lucky was found by an adult and he eventually made a full recovery, but the indifferent response of the pupils says much about our frozen emotions towards a teacher who could be unpredictable and frightening.

Being taught by teachers who were screamers (and belters) was bad enough but in Fairview House, Saggy used temper and sexual shaming to control the girls. She lost her temper for any minor infringement of rules, often only obvious to her, and she would pick on certain girls more than others. If she was taunted by one of the ladies in the village, who mentioned that a girl boarder looked untidy or even worse, smelt, she would return in a steaming rage and take it out on the first girl she encountered. She hated our developing bodies and emerging sexuality, and it was this she used to isolate and attack her victims. Even within our culture of neglect, I thought Saggy often crossed a boundary. Amongst my form was an American girl, in the care of her father, a single parent who worked in the oil industry nearby. Eliza had not been brought up as a British schoolgirl and still clung to the belief that children had rights. When Saggy screamed at Eliza, 'You'll grow up to be a tart like your mother,' she complained to her father, who took his concerns to the head teacher, a man we called the Boss. Evidence was gathered, including mine, and Saggy was hurried into retirement. We had not told our parents about Saggy in our weekly letters home, of if we did, we minimised our fear and pretended the incidents were funny. Parents who had been at boarding school themselves would have roared with laughter, recognising and enjoying the archetype of the bullying matron. Jokes were our habitual means of coping but making light of everything was often used as a means to protect our parents; they were paying so much for our place at this fine school, we couldn't possibly risk upsetting or disappointing them. It might seem contradictory, but we also couldn't risk being removed. We had lost our place within the community, our former friends had moved on to new secondary schools, had settled into friendship groups and wouldn't accept us back. Anyway, being at home was uncomfortable, because we couldn't find within ourselves the child who had left, yet it was that child our parents expected us to be. It was far better to stay where we were.

In the 1960s, adult rage was common and expected. It was not unusual to have direct contact with four or five adults with unregulated emotions, as I did during my time in education. I have already highlighted what may have gone wrong in individual families and for those who suffered trauma during military service. Anyone witnessing the horrors of war would return harmed, even with mental health difficulties, but was there the additional possibility of widespread, generational trauma? The 1960s were close to the end of the Second World War, although to my peer group it already felt like history. Our teachers and parents had shared a common experience. Many had been children during the war and may have worried about fathers or brothers who were fighting. Their mothers may have lost a son or husband and were emotionally absent for their surviving children, due to unresolved, complex grief. There was for some the daily terror of enemy raids and the fear of nights spent in bomb shelters. Others would have been sent to live with strangers through evacuation or were fearful that they might be evacuated. Whatever their individual circumstances, all wartime children, however far they were from the centre of conflict, would have been raised by parents who were afraid. Meeting the emotional needs of their children must have seemed like a low priority, when they faced an uncertain future, possibly under Nazi occupation. Our grandparents' inability to provide adequate containment, due to their own fears, may well have left behind a generation unable to control their emotions, or support the emotional development of their own children – my 1960s peer group.

Observing adults during an unregulated meltdown, or watching another child being hit, harms children because the teacher and classroom become unsafe. My friend Oliver was often pulled from class to be given the tawse by the Boss. One of the qualities expected of a Scottish head teacher in the 1960s was a unique competence in inflicting pain. At my boarding school, only the head of rugby was able to compete at the Boss's level. When Oliver returned to his seat at our shared desk, he trembled, forcing his reddened hands under his armpits and struggling not to cry. I glanced at him, twisting my mouth in sympathy but then stared straight ahead, saying nothing. A hug would only have made the situation worse for us both and anyway, I wouldn't have known how to give one.

For a child at boarding school, isolated from parents and home and seeking security wherever it can be found, the impact of watching emotional abuse or physical punishment is even more profound than it is for a child who attends day school and lives with their family. For the boarding school child, told they are amongst the privileged few, there is nowhere to turn for help, nowhere to share worries about what they have seen. Their only outlet is to retreat into denial, humour and the avoidant profile so valued by this culture.

CHAPTER 5

The Girls

We were a large form of ten girls, which was unusual in Fairview, and we dominated the house, or at least believed we did, because of our subtle but steady non-cooperation with rules, at least until Saggy left. Four of us had started as boarders the year before, two of us in Rosehill, two of us in Fairview, and we were already hardened against homesickness. We made no allowance at all, and in my case didn't even notice the separation grief of the other six girls. While we were acutely aware of each other's presence in our confined form room, monitoring our own actions and words as well as theirs, we were certainly not watching out for each other's emotions.

Mood swings were common and it was not unusual for us to complain bitterly behind each other's backs, or to end up on the receiving end of silent treatment, but emotional outbursts, anger or open displays of frustration were rare. Even when anger would have been expected and fair, for example when I betrayed Beth by going out with a boy who was supposed to be her boyfriend, she was cool with me, but there were no harsh words or tears.

One Monday in May, during my fourth year, I recorded in my diary, 'Martha and Beatrice are bitches. They've been ganging up on me all weekend. I haven't spoken to Beatrice for two days. Not a word in the dormitory. And Beth told *me* I was a bitch.' But only a few days later I played a card game with Beth, and by the following Saturday, Martha and I rushed out of Fairview after breakfast to meet boys in the cafe. Although apologies were rare, most incidents were quickly forgotten, because we simply had to cooperate.

Within the boarding house, I tried out a role of being funny and making others laugh. This was only partially successful, and I often misjudged the mood. I valued my quick wit and rarely missed an opportunity to make a quip at another girl's expense. If I had any excuse, it would have been that the jibe was funny. I wouldn't have been aware that it was preferable to let a clever remark pass, rather than hurt another girl's feelings. Like many girls who are insecure about relationships, I struggled when I was the target of hurtful comments or silent treatment. If I overheard whispers in corners, or was the object of a brief flash of anger, I assumed it was all about me. Even when I learned the truth, or the moment passed, I wasn't able to build on my experience to try and become less self-centred about relationships. I was slow to make secure or long-term friendships perhaps because other girls were wary of me. It is hardly surprising that after my primary school experience, making friends was a low priority. I didn't trust other girls.

Apart from two original Fairview girls who started school together in Mr Q's class, our friendships were rarely permanent or deep but because of this, we were flexible about which girl we spent time with. During my first few years in Fairview, I was close with Martha, because we made each other laugh, but by fourth year, she had drifted away, preferring to be friends with Beatrice. With hindsight, this was surprising, since we both had boyfriends in sixth year and would have benefitted from a trusting friendship that allowed us to swap notes. Equally surprising was how little outward reaction I showed. From my dramatic diary entries, I was deeply troubled by her rejection but the importance of not showing any emotion or making a fuss in front of others was my priority.

Throughout my time at Fairview, we walked to school in the same pair or threesome. This was part of the house culture, passed down from generation to generation. Even after the original friendship had passed, or if we had fallen out with the girls we walked with, no girl was left isolated. In the mornings we would gather in the cloakroom, which smelt of damp raincoats and rubber, our mood characteristically sombre at this time of day, and wait for our walking partner. This custom and practice helped to resolve hard feelings, since it was difficult to hold on to a grievance and ignore the girl by your side, if you had to walk beside them all the way to school.

Fairview should have been our safe space from the judgement of boys and the weighty academic expectations of our teachers, but the imbalance in numbers between boy and girl boarders, and our sense of privilege at being one of a tiny minority of girl boarders, meant that we were in competition with each other academically and for the attention of the boys. If I asked for help with maths exercises or French grammar, it would have been given, but there was absolutely no sharing of schoolwork. One episode of silent treatment directed at me happened because a drawing of mine was similar to another girls' homework. The plagiarism was unintentional, possibly even unconscious, but my denial was useless, since being a liar was a worse crime than being a cheat.

The girls could be horribly disloyal beyond the walls of the boarding house, reflecting the patriarchal culture of the school, where boys' interests and values dominated. To make the boys laugh, Fairview girls would happily share personal details about other girl boarders. As for me, it was sharing details about how I looked in the morning without make-up. If the boys mimicked a girl boarder, we would laugh and join in. We accepted as true their deep-seated misogynistic views about individual girls and women in general. When one of my form became the victim of nasty, sexual innuendo, she quickly assumed Fairview girls were the source, rather than the boyfriend she loved. The scandal had not originated from us – we had heard the gossip and had tried to defend her – but such was her cynicism about our loyalty, we were never able to convince her we hadn't let her down.

Any assumption that girl boarders would be better able than boys to look after or care for each other was a myth. Because we didn't value ourselves, we judged each other by the standards of the patriarchy. When Beth and

I had a rare conversation about sex and boyfriends, I felt uncomfortable afterwards and wrote, 'I may have told her too much. I don't know if she is to be trusted.'

Why was there a girls' boarding house at all? The inconvenience for parents of having sons and daughters at separate schools was minimal. It is hard not to conclude that we were there for the benefit of the boy boarders, to provide heterosexual sexual experience and the mothering they needed. Since we weren't much good at either of these, it's hardly surprising the boy boarders seemed to resent us. In my diary, I recorded a conversation with two boys, Henry and Steven, who told me that Marie was not like other Fairview girls. When I asked what was different about her, they laughed and said she was a 'mummy'. What the boys unconsciously saw in Marie was a girl who would nurture them. As a late starter, Marie had not yet formed the boarding school personality we shared, one which frustrated and disappointed the boys. Shaped by three or four years as boarders, the Fairview girls were emotionally inhibited, self-reliant and not easily impressed by a boy's need to be looked after.

If Fairview girls rarely shared secrets and could be cruel and disloyal, we were able to communicate: 'Barbara and I talked for hours about what's wrong with the school and the house.' Free from the disapproval of the boys and our teachers, our behaviour often involved minor rule-breaking pranks and dissolving into side-splitting laughter. In a diary entry from sixth form, I wrote, 'We put out the lights in the study and chased each other around, laughing like mad.' On one, more serious, occasion, we let off fireworks from the dormitory window: 'It's all round the school. Some think it's funny, others don't, including teachers. At least I was only spectating.' Naturally, we were all gated (confined to the house) the following weekend.

We chose to be ignorant about each other's lives at home. Although we knew the place where each girl lived and the basic details of her family, such as how many siblings she had or what her parents' jobs were, we never spoke in detail about our families. It was too risky to share fears about a parent's health, their failing marriages or their redundancies, in case we made the error of showing emotion. Worse, the details might be spread around the school by the following day. When one of our form returned from a phone call with her parents about the birth of a new sibling, she cried openly. We offered no sympathy, looking down at our schoolbooks or comics until she had recovered. The safe birth of a new baby is a joyful event but to a child at boarding school, it is another change, a significant regrouping of parenting and resources, without their presence. To the baby, the older sibling will become an easily forgotten visitor, and for the boarding school child it is impossible to build a secure relationship with a sibling who changes and develops between every holiday. We understood none of this because we were children, and if we had been asked about her reaction, might have explained that she shouldn't have cried because mother and baby were well. Parents of children at boarding school, particularly young children under thirteen, need to be sensitive to the child's need for continuity at home. It is not wise to bring a new puppy into the household as soon as the child is out of the door, to make big changes to the home or take the remaining children on a special holiday, no matter how tempting. My own family moved house often but, due to finances rather than insight into child development, kept everything the same in the new house, including carpets and curtains, and this helped us to adjust.

There were times when the girls in my form spoke to each other with brutal honesty, and if it was my turn to have my character ripped to shreds, I recorded the shock and rage in my diary but told no one. The rationale was that if your friends didn't tell you where you were going wrong, you might never learn. In December of our fourth year, a friend said to me that I was 'nasty, dull and had lost my personality'. She then went on to explain why I had become like this, including the fact that I was hanging around with girls from the year below. If anyone said such things to me now, I'd cry for days but I accepted some of what she said as true, probably the bit about me being nasty, and the rest I robustly denied to my diary. Such harsh moments of truth were common between us.

Living so closely together, it was highly likely any one of us might become tiresome to the others. Wary of risking an emotional outburst, we would discuss this girl at length behind her back, then one of us would volunteer to tell her what everyone thought. If caught on the receiving end of advice, it was important to take these talks well, since a show of emotion would only confirm the low opinion of the group. Once the advice had been given, relationships would settle for a while, until the next candidate developed annoying habits.

My friend's harsh summative report included an important observation; somewhere in primary school, probably in my move from England to Scotland, I had been accelerated a year, a mistake perpetuated on that walk from the church hall back to the junior school building. My 'high-flier' status was an accident because I certainly wasn't exceptionally bright, and my parents didn't seem to know when or how it had happened. Amongst the girls in my form, I was younger in every way: physically, emotionally and in terms of overall maturity. My teenage brain was going through its dramatic reorganisation a year behind theirs and my puberty, slow anyway, was dragging behind. Compared to girls I thought of as 'really clever', I felt silly and inadequate and found more genial friends amongst younger girls in the form below. If there ever was an argument against accelerating pupils at school, I was proof.

Living within our enforced togetherness, throughout every day and night, our 'home' could never be a place of safety or relaxation. It was impossible to be alone, especially as we couldn't access the dormitory during the day. A behaviour common amongst adult ex-boarders is to feel like an outsider in groups, to always watch and monitor from the edge. This characteristic is embedded at boarding school where escape is impossible and watching, monitoring and judging each other is necessary for survival. A social miscalculation might resonate for the rest of a girl's time at school and had to be avoided. Noise, bustle and hypervigilance, combined with exacting academic standards, managing largely unsupervised sexual relationships, coping alone with period pains, and avoiding the ire of the matron or housemistress, inevitably led to moments of feeling overwhelmed. While we could not escape physically, or risk showing emotion in the form of tears or temper, we could free our minds from the group, creating another behavioural habit – dissociation – that would persist throughout our adult lives whenever things became difficult. On the Saturday Marie disappeared from the form room and spent all day in an empty bathtub, she had clearly had enough of us all and was suffering from overwhelm. Together in the form room, crushed onto the few armchairs, or sitting on the metal storage heater, we talked about her, listing her faults, even sharing that she was having a difficult time, but no one checked to see if she wanted to talk. When she reappeared, nothing was said.

The girl boarders were friendly but not friends, close but watchful, interested but not concerned, almost like sisters, but without any family loyalty. Sisters are not always friends, even as adults, since family dynamics, injustice and favouritism can rankle for many years, but in later life, once the parents are gone, many sisters do find a deep friendship. This was not possible for us, having no family ties. Once we left school, we maintained little contact beyond Christmas cards or reunions organised by the school. In Fairview, we had been thrown together by chance rather than choice and for our everyday well-being and sanity, we simply had to get along. We were heroes of tolerance, but apart from a few exceptions, failed to forge the lifelong friendships often valued by those who attended all-girls' boarding schools.

CHAPTER 6

The Dormitory

I missed being with older girls at night. In Rosehill, we'd all slept together in one long dormitory, and the younger girls had been treated with benign indifference. The seniors jumped on us only if they noticed we'd stepped out of line, when Moira and I were caught trying to leave the house without Kate. Otherwise, we were ignored. Our invisibility allowed for profitable watching and listening: how a bra was worn, what you should allow a boy to 'do' or whether you were still a virgin if you used Tampax. One of the older Rosehill girls saved us from the ordeal of stockings and suspenders by persuading her mum to buy armloads of tights from Mary Quant, which she passed around. My stockings dragged at my suspender belt, pulling it down over my skinny hips, so that by the end of the day I waddled home with stocking tops resting just above my knees and the suspender belt only held in place by the gusset of my substantial navy knickers. By contrast, thick, cable-knit tights felt like a reassuring hug. The senior girls' boyfriends reacted badly to the new tights. I didn't understand why, although I heard that some girls went on wearing stockings and suspenders because their boyfriends preferred them.

Someone must have looked only at my date of birth, because in my first term at Fairview I was placed in a dormitory in the eaves of the house, with the youngest girls. I didn't appreciate hearing new girls sobbing themselves to sleep and tried to ignore them. My own vulnerability was only just under control and I didn't want to acknowledge another child's distress. One of the new boarders, a tiny girl with two older brothers in the school, showed her feelings by aiming punches at me as I tried to sleep. I complained to the housemistress, hoping that telling on a new 'bug' wouldn't do any harm. Within weeks, I was moved into a large eight-bedded dormitory with my own form. The dormitories were not comfortable places, with the same dull linoleum and bare walls as the downstairs common rooms. Bedspreads added some colour, and our soft toys parodied a child's bedroom. Allowing boarders to bring a teddy bear to school represented the full spectrum of the school's approach to emotional well-being and must have impressed our parents.

Before slipping into our icy beds, we had to face the bathroom routine. We undressed in the dormitory but always wore a dressing gown and slippers to walk to the bathroom, despite having to strip naked at the sinks. If your name wasn't on the bath rota, you had to strip-wash – a ritual supervised by one of the matrons. With a facecloth (regulation, named), we lined up in the fridge-like room, the windows always wide open against odours. First, we washed our faces, then rinsed and wrung out the cloth. Then, we rubbed the facecloth across a rock-hard bar of green soap and scrubbed under our arms and between our legs.

Facecloths were new to me. At home I had a bath every night, the water frothing with generous amounts of Matey, and used a dripping sponge to mop at my face. These facecloths, which I learned must be treated with reverence, hung in rows above the white, porcelain sinks, becoming steadily more rancid until they were boil-washed on a Friday. I begged other girls to let me have their bath. Even the tepid, shallow water we were allowed helped me feel warmer in bed. 'Hotties', or hot water bottles, were delivered to each dormitory in baskets, their knitted covers smelling of generations of unwashed feet. Clutching one of these, already warm rather than hot, was our bedtime comfort, much like Harlow's monkeys. Watching the film of Harlow's 1950s experiments with baby monkeys separated from their mothers is heartbreaking, but it was an important early example of how young mammals seek warmth and comfort from a cloth-covered mother substitute in preference to a wire substitute who provided them with milk. At eleven, going on twelve, we were beyond the developmental stage of clinging to our mothers, but broken attachments had caused us to regress. Under the covers, knitted hotties had to substitute for our mothers.

In a school report, I was described as becoming 'over-excited' at bedtime. This was an understatement. I was often hyper-aroused, jumping around, showing off and being silly. Overwhelmed by anxiety that had been held in check for hours, it was my worst time of day. I would leap across beds, sing, dance or create a tableau from the soft toys. These were ignored, and when I insisted the others look, no one found them funny, including one where I pretended two teddies were having sex. For no reason at all, I climbed out of the dormitory window onto the roof of an annexe below, landing on the wet, dirty, roofing felt in my slippers and pyjamas. I rapped on the frosted panes of a bathroom window, and from inside, startled girls allowed me to climb over taps and sinks onto the floor. I grinned, waved cheerfully, and escaped through the door, barging back into my dormitory, shouting 'Hello!', my pyjamas filthy and wet with slime and moss.

'Oh, you're back,' they said. If I'd been caught, I would have been gated for weeks and no one was impressed. As it was, I had to scrub the stains out of my pyjamas by hand and for several nights wear damp and increasingly mildewed nightwear.

Once the lights were out, under a blanket and quilt that felt insubstantial, I would lie awake for hours, watchful and listening, with a sense of not being 'tucked in' or held. In the morning, my mood was always low, as was the case with most of my peers. The dormitory was a quiet, solemn place when we dressed for the day.

Because we were girls at boarding school and had read Enid Blyton, we felt obliged to have a midnight feast. After we had decided on a date, we chose the food, bending our heads together over a list, quarrelling, laughing and teasing, as we added to or crossed out suggestions. We didn't have much cash, only our pocket money, which had to be saved for the special night. Some girls went home the weekend before the feast and raided their family's store cupboard.

The food had to be hidden; behind books or pencil cases in our lockers, underneath socks and pyjamas in bedside drawers, or in the cloakroom, dropped into our wellington boots. This was the time of greatest risk and the peak of our excitement. If the food was discovered, everything would be confiscated, and we would be gated as punishment.

On the night of the feast, everything had to be carried upstairs. Lookouts monitored the matron's forays between dormitory and bathroom, signalling to girls waiting on the dark stairs with armloads of biscuits, crisps and sweets whether it was safe to come up. If the matron was in a bad mood, she might notice that some girls hadn't rushed upstairs when bedtime was called, and other girls, those first in the dormitory, had since disappeared. Whatever her mood, it was important to keep the matron chatting and this task was assigned to any girl known to be skilled at manipulating adults with earnest questions and the ability to fake interest in the replies.

Once the food was stashed away in the dormitory, into lockers or under beds, we were unusually cooperative about getting under the covers. Someone who owned an alarm clock would set it for midnight, and once the lights were out we pulled our quilts over our heads, not risking whispering or giggling in case we alerted a matron listening at the door. Being woken abruptly in the dark, after only a few hours' sleep, felt cold and disorienting. There were no giggles, no suppressed laughter or bright eyes shining above hands cupping a smiling mouth. Instead, lonely girls silently chewed on sweet food they didn't want and when enough honour had been given to the ritual, we rolled over, said goodnight, and went back to sleep amongst the crumbs of our picnic. Amongst my peer group, one midnight feast was enough and no more were organised. This wasn't a deliberate choice, more a lack of enthusiasm. By our fourth year, the fun we had discovered in making plans found a new outlet in assignations with boys or illicit trips to the cities of Edinburgh and Glasgow.

*

In Fairview, the dormitory was where bullying happened. After lights out, we were on our own until the morning. In my first year, we had to endure 'truths' nights, a practice new to former Rosehill boarders, but apparently familiar to our companions from Fairview. The principle was this: each girl took a turn telling one other girl what was unlikeable about her. As the girls' breathing settled into rhythm of sleep, I hoped the dreaded moment had passed but too late, the peace was broken by a voice from the dark, 'I know, let's have a truths' night.'

More dominant girls were unwilling to hear any personal criticism and would start arguing, countering the accusations with criticisms of their own. Inevitably, the same girls were always chosen to hear unwelcome 'truths'. If I was late to have a turn, already smarting from the unkind things I had heard about me, I made up the nastiest truth I could manage, even if it wasn't true. At this point, I hadn't learned to be funny. These games disappeared after our first few months as the newcomers became more confident. It was easy to feign sleep or turn over and refuse to play. It's hard to play a truths night game on your own and trying to push this torment onto others became its own truth: no one likes you because you keep on suggesting truths nights.

For the first few nights in my new dormitory, as I lay in the dark listening to my companions settle, I was poked with a ruler. At first, I tolerated this, kicking out and pretending to laugh, but eventually I tired of the game and waited to catch them crawling across the floor towards my bed. I was useless at fighting but had the right stance and language, an unexpected social advantage over my companions who had attended more civilised primary schools. In fact, I already had a reputation as a fighter, having wasted no time in showing off my skills when a boy in my junior class had tried to snatch a bag of sweets out of my hand. When I raised my fists and threatened my tormentors with a fight, they crawled away and the poking stopped.

One of the girls in our dormitory was a victim of severe bullying, the worst I witnessed in Fairview. She was in the year below us and had been ostracised by her own peer group, which may have been why she slept in a different dormitory. Iona was an ordinary little girl but deeply unhappy at boarding school, often tearful and open about her loneliness, which made her vulnerable to teasing and ridicule. The open impatience and intolerance shown towards Iona by the staff would certainly have fuelled the bullying. Although I saw little of her through the day, at night I stood by as she was called names, her belongings were moved or taken, and her bed messed up when she tried to get ready for bed. Of course, she cried and begged them to stop. Only the year before, I'd been the target of bullying and knew exactly what was happening, but I said nothing. Survival was all that mattered in this new environment, and I was determined to save myself. If I had intervened to help Iona, we both would have been lost. This miserable fate must be Iona's alone.

One night, a girl told the assistant matron her purse was missing. The dormitory was searched and it was found in Iona's locker. She sobbed and protested her innocence, arguing that the purse had been planted. The following day, there was an 'investigation'. I was terrified the spotlight would fall on me because of my shoplifting. When it was my turn to be interviewed, I told the truth: I had seen Iona move something from her pyjama case to her locker, but I couldn't be sure what it was. I paused, waiting for the accusation that I had stolen the purse but nothing was said. Was it possible that the reason I had become a boarder so suddenly was a secret kept between my parents and the Boss?

Iona's parents were persuaded to take her home, under the pretext that she wasn't 'boarding school material' or some other patronising phrase used to justify the school's failure to keep a child safe. The day Iona's parents came to collect her, they paused in our schoolroom, the mother's pale, tear-stained face echoing that other mother from my primary school. She tore into us for the harm we had done to her little girl but I felt no shame, no responsibility, and stared at the floor until the blaming words stopped. In the ringing silence that followed their departure, we looked at each other, our faces pale, blank, our stomachs hollow, but said nothing. I reached into my locker to find my book.

Iona had an older sister in the boarding house. Why hadn't she stepped in to protect her sibling? By this time, I also had an older sister in Fairview. My sister was moved from her state secondary school, where she was thriving, the year after my own unfortunate start. Both Iona's sister and mine were seniors, so we never met. They had their own dormitories and studies and even ate in a separate dining room. Mixing across year groups was not encouraged but my sister and I did try and meet every few days in a small downstairs toilet that smelt of disinfectant, always icy cold from the open window. We didn't ask about well-being, or friends, or schoolwork but reminded each other of our absent family by grumbling about our parents.

I was no longer a 'new' girl when I moved into Fairview, but my sister was. It didn't occur to me to check whether Peggy had settled, because I was fine. She was my big sister, and, in my eyes, invulnerable. At thirteen, she had the resilience of an adolescent already forging new attachments away from her parents. Her separation from home would not have been equivalent to the suffering of a child of seven or eight but, nevertheless, it was still hard. She was never bullied, but the girls in her form resented a bright newcomer and she was often called 'swot', because she had to work hard to keep up with self-promoting, 'clever' students. Fortunately, there was another new starter, an escapee from a girls' convent school. Deprivation is relative and to Sheelagh, compared to her convent Fairview was a nurturing, luxurious environment, with warm and compassionate staff. There were ex-Rosehill girls too, also strangers to Fairview but already confident boarders, who welcomed them both.

*

Bullying rarely happens in isolation; there are always bystanders who actively join in, ignore the bullying, or fail to help the target child, even when they are perfectly aware of what is happening. That was my role with Iona. Bullying is now taken seriously by schools and there has been success with whole-school programmes that focus on an anti-bullying culture. From an early age, small children are encouraged to recognise and name emotions, to think about how other children are feeling and to tell an adult whenever anything feels uncomfortable.

Recognising how difficult it is for a bullying child to act alone, work with bystanders can help to stop an active bullying situation. These empathy-based programmes are designed to help mediate between the bystanders and the target child, to encourage bystanders to take responsibility, to change their perceptions of the target child and to stop the bullying forever by isolating the bully's behaviour.

In the 1960s, most teachers and parents considered bullying to be a 'normal' part of childhood. Parents who sent their children to boarding school during this and previous decades must have known that their child was at risk of being bullied, at any time of the day or night, without the protection of adults, and were willing to pay for the privilege. This was certainly true of parents who had been boarders themselves, convinced that bullying had done them no harm and had, in fact, been character-forming. This wasn't true of my parents, or those of my peer group, since, apart from my father, we were not from a tradition of ex-boarder families. Our parents were guilty of an unthinking trust in the institution and a lack of interest in their child's life. We didn't tell them the truth because we cared for their innocence and wanted to protect them. Besides, Iona's fate made it clear what would happen if you risked telling. Like her, we might be blamed for being a victim and sent home.

I regret that in the boarding house, I took part in many incidents, often in the dormitory, in the role of active or passive bystander during bullying episodes. At the time, we passed these off as jokes or teasing, such as making a girl's bed so that she couldn't get under the sheets or by hiding someone's glasses. Each one of us suffered these humiliations from time to time, forced to find the energy to laugh no matter how you were feeling. It must have been so much worse for girls who were frequent victims. Had they known, would our parents have been happy to pay for this? But they did not know, we never told them, accepting such treatment as part of the privilege our parents had chosen for us.

Due to the intrusive access of social media, modern children face the same dilemma boarders have always faced. There is no longer any safe space where a child can escape their tormentors, unless their parents are willing to take a firm stand at home over access to devices. Sadly, bullying hasn't diminished, particularly in secondary schools. In 2018, a survey of secondary school teachers indicated that incidents of bullying had doubled in the five years since 2013, with many pupils reporting that they had been bullied on social media. It is essential that anti-bullying programmes in schools continue to be a priority. This work will never be finished.

CHAPTER 7

The Boys

Pupils at all-boys boarding schools in the 1960s faced bullying, corporal punishment and the particularly nasty combination of sexual bullying, perpetrated in all its variety by older pupils upon younger boys. Co-ed schools, particularly co-ed boarding schools, were thought to be the answer. Girls would give boys the mothering, mentoring and friendship they needed, as well as satisfying their sexual needs. Was it was acceptable to include girls at a boys' school as an answer to boys' problems, without considering the unique needs of the girls? One ex-boarder has written to me to say, 'There was no plan for the girls ... they just opened a boarding house and put us in it'.

Most of the boys' houses were run by an unmarried male teacher, an assistant housemaster and a matron, living in the same environment as we did: spartan conditions, unappetising food and biting cold, although their spaces to play and play equipment were better than ours. Unlike girl boarders, boys were exposed to corporal punishment both in the boarding house and at school. The belt or tawse might happen out of the blue as a result of a teacher's explosive unregulated state, or at the other end of the scale, for minor rule-breaking, such as forgetting plimsolls for PE. Our school was no different from any other at this time, whether boarding or day, private or state. Corporal punishment was common in all Scottish schools in the 1960s, only being finally banned in 1987 in state schools and 2000 in private schools.

As well as the belt, in the boarding houses boys were 'slippered' for typical rule-breaking. This meant bending over the housemaster's knee to be 'spanked' with a carpet slipper, often with a senior boy or prefect in attendance. Facing corporal punishment, or even the threat of being hit, must have been terrifying for small boys, separated for the first time from their families. An ex-boarder has told me that when he was only ten, he was given six strokes of the tawse. Despite the exceptional pain, he managed not to cry and was lauded for his self-control. New boys who cried at night for the first few days or weeks, or worse, wet the bed, often became victims of teasing or ridicule, whereas in Fairview they were generally ignored. Like the girls, young boys were praised for not crying, or showing any other emotional response and most learned to suppress their feelings in order to fit in.

For the boys, girl boarders were an exotic and terrifying cohort, the younger boys incredibly naïve about sex or girls' normal development. Boys who managed to find a girlfriend were expected to report back and most felt honour-bound to make something up, out of insecurity or self-preservation, rather than being malicious about the girl. In adolescence, many boy boarders found Fairview girls shuttered and closed off, protected within a hard, defensive personality that leaned towards nastiness, and were wary of approaching us.

One benefit of co-education in our earliest years, when we were still children rather than adolescents, was that girls and boys formed close, natural friendships. In my junior year, I met Oliver, already friends with the American girl, Eliza. While Mr Q was engrossed in his *Glasgow Herald*, they passed me a drawing they'd been working on all morning. The picture showed a naked woman with her legs spread and hands tied, suspended by a frame over an open fire. I pretended to admire the artwork, since that seemed like a safe bet, but didn't understand what the picture was about. I don't think Eliza was the instigator. I knew her well once she became a boarder at Fairview and she never showed any particular interest in violent, misogynist sex, or even sex at all. This was my first encounter with Oliver, an unhappy child who comfortably broke the unwritten rule that we shouldn't speak about our families.

I liked Oliver's honesty about his parents but wasn't sure if he was being truthful. I had never before heard a child say his parents didn't want him at home, especially his father. I shared nothing about myself. We stayed friends for the first two years of secondary school, often sitting next to each other in lessons because of the alphabetical order of our names. Oliver's neediness was his downfall. In our senior years, we didn't meet outside school, except in the cafes where he hung around on the edge of a group of boys who openly disliked him and called him 'fat boy', which he wasn't. I always spoke to him, even offered to sew a button onto his coat, trying to give him a little of the mothering he needed but I couldn't pretend that I didn't prefer other boys. In my fourth year, he badly let me down and our friendship ended. This is covered in a later chapter on sexual bullying.

Steven was a shy child, with a warm smile and a keen sense of humour. In the art rooms, illuminated by skylights and smelling of paint, linseed oil and clay, we were allowed to talk quietly as we worked. We never spoke about our lives beyond school, so I knew almost nothing about him – where his home was, who was in his family, what his interests were – but I did know his father had died. Outside art classes, Steven and I had no contact but by fourth or fifth year, he hovered on the edge of a group of boys from his boarding house who met Fairview girls after school and at weekends.

As far as girls like me were concerned, there were two types of boys, those in our class, who were friends, and the older boys we hoped would notice us. In my mind, Steven was firmly in the 'friend' camp. Our attempt to form a different sort of relationship was a disaster and my diary entries are a grim reminder of my shocking lack of empathy. We lost everything, respect for each other as well as friendship, but my only concern was the impact our break-up might have on my popularity.

The beginnings of empathy can be seen in babies as young as one year old but for children raised by adults who are emotionally young, who cannot handle their own feelings, never mind those of their children, the development of empathy will be a struggle. Through modelling from parents and teachers, children learn that feelings have names and that most people feel the same emotions in similar circumstances. 'Good enough' parenting helps a child feel understood and able to trust that their emotions are noticed and accepted without judgement. Given time and the right emotional care, most children will learn to empathise with others. My behaviour towards Steven suggests I was very late to develop empathy and perhaps not until I had children of my own.

I was capable of being less than kind to boys I hardly knew. For one year, in chemistry, I sat next to a day boy called Nicky and we were paired for experiments. I was bored, and messed around with our equipment, ignoring his protests. The more he reacted, the more I laughed. There was nothing about Nicky that made me want to wreck his experiments. It happened simply because I wasn't interested and he was. There were no bystanders, the bullying was not personal, nor did it persist outside the lesson we shared. This situation didn't need a restorative justice level of intervention, but a teacher who noticed, separated us, and gave me a suitable punishment. Later, I learned that Nicky had a scholarship and if he failed any subjects, the award, and therefore his school place, was at risk. Scholarship students faced unimagined pressure; not for them the luxury of messing around in lessons, or even coasting, in the way most other pupils took for granted. The girl boarders faced similar pressures, knowing how rare it was to gain a place in our single boarding house and how expensive our education. I cared about doing well and what my school place cost my parents, but I never had to face worries like Nicky's. We should have known these things about each other. Now I do know, I am sorry and feel grateful my immaturity didn't extend beyond that one year when he was unlucky enough to share chemistry lessons with me.

There were many boys at school who were safe and worth knowing. Steven managed to walk the fine line of being popular and included while never taking part in the verbal harassment of girls. So why did I seek out critical, 'difficult' boys? This makes perfect sense within the context of attachment theory. In the company of boys who could be unkind and manipulative, I found the drama I craved and worked hard to seek their approval. I wasn't particularly popular, but I was one of the crowd, which was all that mattered.

*

The boys stuck together in groups from their boarding houses, and we often met the same few boys every day for weeks or months, then changed to a different crew. If the girls made the switch, the boys were furious and accused us of making fools of ourselves. Didn't we know we were being laughed at? Didn't we know those other boys were embarrassed by us hanging around? If we were dumped, we felt the shock and pain of betrayal but took our dislike out on the girls, usually younger, who had replaced us. If they were Fairview girls, they would have felt the full silent treatment.

Outside weekend afternoons and evenings when we could use the club, in our senior years we met boy boarders in one of two cafes which served the village. The Teapot had existed for decades, a gloomy back room with a jukebox which no one could afford to play. There were sticky, plastic bench seats around the walls, facing laminated tables and a hatch to the kitchen, where a cook slaved over fry-ups and bacon sandwiches. To a hungry girl boarder, the smell could be either mouth-watering or nauseating, depending upon the age of the fat and where we were in our monthly cycle. The other cafe, Tangs, was above a dress and jewellery shop. It was airy, with tall windows and Scandinavian furniture. In Tangs, we bought hot Ribena and Club biscuits, and I became expert at folding and shaping the wrapper back into the mould of the biscuit, to trick any boy who tried to snatch it. We shared the cafes with the village on an unspoken rota. We crowded the space with our loud voices after school, and never saw anyone from the village in either cafe. Local youths too young for the pub waited for us to disappear in the evening before crowding the Teapot. By three o'clock, women from the village glanced at their watches and hurried away from Tangs. Until the club opened, we owned both cafes until teatime, even at weekends.

In whichever cafe we chose, we were an audience for the boys and, being typical adolescents, much of their talk was about girls. Regardless of our presence, they shared details about the sexual behaviour of other girls, information they swore was true, facts gathered from the girls' actual boyfriends. If we didn't know the girl, we laughed out loud, but if she was from Fairview, we felt awkward at not defending her but also relief they weren't laughing at us. The price of being included was to accept that girls had to be mocked, our femaleness was up for ridicule. To succeed with boys, we must be sexually attractive and available while holding out against too much sex. This felt like a difficult balance to achieve, but for some reason, it was our sole responsibility. Girls who had a boyfriend but had successfully resisted sex were 'frigid', but any girl who had willingly participated in sex, and heaven forbid, enjoyed it, was called a 'tart'. Girls who chose to avoid mixing with the boys at all were designated 'trolls'.

If this sex business seemed like a difficult game to play for girls learning about their role for the first time, such prejudices and bias were not new and still persist. But for girls isolated from their families, the problem lay in not hearing any other version of ourselves except this misogynistic view. In a good enough 1960s home, most parents valued their daughter for her attributes and strengths and, at least within his daughter's earshot, the father would have modelled respect for women.

The National Education Union and UK Feminista published a study in 2017 called 'It's Just Everywhere', a study on sexism in schools and how we tackle it. Here are the summary findings:

- Sexism in schools is endemic – but it is not inevitable. Consistent and ongoing action is required from schools, government and education bodies to tackle it.

- Sexual harassment is highly prevalent in schools. It is also gendered, overwhelmingly involving boys targeting girls.

- The use of misogynistic language is commonplace in schools.

- Gender stereotyping is a typical feature of school culture, often reinforced through mundane, 'everyday' actions.

- Sexism and sexual harassment in schools has been normalised and is rarely reported.

The 'It's Just Everywhere' report appeared only six years ago. Girls at co-ed boarding schools today will be as much at risk of sexist attitudes and stereotyping from boy boarders as we were in the 1960s. They must be regarded as an at risk group within the boarding community and active measures taken by the school to counteract a culture of misogyny, with relationship education for boys and girls, close monitoring of peer-on-peer friendships by staff and the provision of protection whenever it is needed.

*

Not all Fairview girls sought attention from boys. Some were sensible enough to protect themselves from the pressure of adolescent males, living a life balanced between the boarding house, school and organised sport. They maintained this triangulation for their entire time at school, which was a safe option, but one that held no attraction for me, a girl obsessed by relationships. By third year, when I turned fourteen, I realised that no one was checking where I was after school or during the empty hours of the weekend. As long as I turned up for meals and at bedtime, I didn't have to spend any time in the boarding house and no one would care. Instead of a sterile common room or muddy games pitch, there were warm cafes where a cup of tea could be bought for a few pence and spun out to last until teatime. Some of the older boys had the same idea and the centre of my life outside lessons, along with several other Fairview girls from my year, switched from the boarding house to socialising in cafes or at the club. If our choice of a male peer group included those who enjoyed rebellion, so much the better.

Our male friends enjoyed subversion, but were not impressed if we tried to join them in breaking rules. We turned up at one of their smoking haunts and were asked to leave, since girls were not supposed to smoke. I wrote in my diary, 'They didn't approve, so I promised I'd stop.' If I have been spared a life as a smoker, I am grateful, but the degree of their control over us was worse than I remembered, without the evidence from my diary. Beatrice and I believed we were good singers and agreed to sing with a newly formed band. The boys we were already hanging around with didn't like this arrangement and we were warned off, threatened with a 'hellish reception' if we went ahead and sang. Of course, we complied, dropping the band as friends as well as singing with them. I didn't ask Beatrice about her feelings, but my anxiety levels soared at being threatened and I was relieved to comply with their demands so that the threats would stop.

When I was with the boys, I wasn't a show-off like in the boarding house, but I couldn't stop myself from making jokes at their expense, mimicking the way they teased each other. This was risky behaviour, since funny women are rarely popular. I developed a reputation for being 'bitchy' and reluctantly had to accept jibes from the cafe gang as payback.

More surprising was the frequency of unexpected and harsh criticism from boys I rarely met, other than in lessons. I recorded these meticulously in my diary, snide remarks about my low intelligence, my poverty of factual knowledge and my slim chance of ever going to university. These are typical of the 'trolling' women now face every day on social media, from men who feel slighted by a woman's ability, particularly if she has drawn attention to her achievements. Even a recent prime minister referred to such women as 'girly swots'. In subjects like English and History, where I met both boarders and day boys who regarded themselves as intellectuals, I would not have hidden my ability. At home, 'clever' was highly valued, regardless of gender, and there was no doubt I was clever in these subjects. But then, as now, a clever girl or woman was seen as a personal insult or challenge to the pride of certain boys.

*

More than girls, boys' friendships tend to occur within hierarchies. There can be a hierarchy for success in sport or music, being brainy, having a unique skill or interest, or any other that boys regard as important at the time. Some boys are lucky enough to achieve across all hierarchies, and have friends in many different camps, but as long as success can be found in one area, he'll do well. Boys who cannot climb the ladder of any hierarchy tend to become disaffected, and those were our friends, a group free from rugby practice, music lessons, or the officers' training corps, and available to spend time with us. A subculture is a useful alternative hierarchy and our friends earned mutual respect by smoking, drinking, growing their hair long or altering their uniforms in ways that annoyed the staff. They wore huge, gaberdine coats that reached the pavement, excessively long scarves or ties knotted to be either short and wide, or long and stringy. They were too nebulous and unstructured to be a 'gang', but for a brief period they regarded themselves as different, and taunted keen, conforming boys with the label 'bourgeois'. Bourgeois boys were those who turned up in first year with briefcases and wore their blazers tightly buttoned, but in the intervening years had become sporty, non-smoking, smartly dressed and unexpectedly handsome. Our boys hated them.

*

Once I had a friendship group outside the boarding house, I stopped envying the day pupils their parents. I had achieved absolute freedom from the control and scrutiny of adults, and as long as I closely followed Fairview rules, I was in charge of my own life. This is the point where my separation from home became absolute; there was no longer anything about home I missed or pined for.

Adolescents will always try to break free from parental control, but from my work with this age group, I've found that they're still proud of their families and secretly enjoy home comforts and mothering. Sensible parents stand by quietly on the sidelines, allowing their son or daughter to feel independent while staying watchful. It is possible for relaxed parents to enjoy their child's teenage years as much as any another phase of development. Adolescents strive for freedom but their need for a mother, father, or both, is every bit as great during the teenage years, as in earlier childhood. To leave adolescents in charge of themselves is an abrogation of parental responsibility, and an even worse failure of care, if those adults are *in loco parentis.*

CHAPTER 8

Sex

Living on a farm, the reproductive act couldn't be missed, since animals engaged in this more than was strictly necessary. I had no idea of sex in relation to myself until I moved to my Scottish primary school at nine. Within a few days, I was surrounded by a group of girls asking me what I 'did'. I told them I liked to ride horses, a mistake, in retrospect, resulting in weeks of jeering that 'Isobel *rode* horses'. I wasn't a gymkhana, pony-club type but like most farm children, there were a couple of ponies at home to saddle up and trot around the fields. At first, I didn't understand what was so funny, but it was obvious that riding horses was a dirty business, and not in a way that involved cleaning tack or mucking out stables.

Our playground throbbed with sexual menace. At break, we played a game like British Bulldog, calling it a name that sounded like the French for 'go free'. The girls opposed the boys and if a boy was caught, he was bundled into the girls' toilets and 'de-breeked', in other words, stripped of his trousers and underwear, if he was wearing any. The same happened to the girls, who would stumble out of the boys' toilets, crying, their knickers around their ankles. I was nimble and made sure I was never caught. In class photos from these two years, several children have dark shadows under their eyes, a sign of troubled and disrupted sleep. It's not difficult to imagine why sex featured so large in our playground culture.

Another animal and sex scenario happened to me at primary school, but this time, a teacher was at fault. At home we had two small dogs, both bitches, who were endlessly on heat because my parents neglected to have them spayed. Before the school leaving age was raised to fifteen, pupils who did not pass the eleven-plus stayed on at primary school for two years of secondary education, so we had a proper PE teacher on the staff, a tall young man who always wore a tracksuit. He kept two large Alsatian dogs, both male, in the back of his car and at break, released them into the playground for exercise before disappearing back inside for coffee. Anyone who knows dogs will be able to guess what happened next. These huge animals headed straight for me, wherever I tried to hide. My panic rose as they searched for me, noses to the ground, tracking the delicious scent of a bitch on heat. Of course, they mounted me, their huge paws on my shoulders and started humping. Surrounded by a cheering, clapping crowd, I tried to laugh and join in, pretending that the dogs were playing, but I was terrified of falling onto the ground. This happened every day until it suddenly ended. I hope an adult noticed and the PE teacher was reprimanded, but since my mother was part of the same secondary school staff, I would have been told. I didn't report him for the same reason that children of my generation rarely told their parents anything. I was afraid it was my fault, there was something about sex, animals and me that I must have encouraged.

In Rosehill, I quickly learned how the female body looked in puberty, about periods, and the intriguing range of tools required to manage both. There were bras of all shapes and sizes and sanitary pads like boats, requiring complicated and uncomfortable harnesses to keep them in place. In 1965, the school was still trying to enforce strict rules, particularly with regard to our sexual behaviour, so Rosehill staff expected us to return as a group from the Saturday night film. Those of us too young to have boyfriends, and girls single by choice or otherwise, had to walk slowly back to the house and wait, shivering, on a street corner until the senior girls straggled in from their various hideaways, tucking in their shirts and straightening their hair. I didn't give a thought to what they did, I simply hated waiting on bitterly cold, frosty nights for them to finish whatever it was.

Usually, the three youngest girls were hustled upstairs by Miss Kent for our baths but one night we were allowed a few extra minutes in the common room. A girl we called Ruby, because of her burnt-auburn hair, put on a record. She started swaying to 'Under the Boardwalk' by the Rolling Stones, eyes closed, hands moving over her hips, and I knew that whatever went on under the boardwalk was the same thing she'd been doing behind the church hall. Ruby opened her eyes, saw me staring and winked. This boardwalk thing would be mine too. It was coming for me.

Our interest in sex wasn't unusual. In the mid-1960s, a sociologist called Royston Lambert and his colleagues interviewed adolescents about their life at boarding school. The children were not specifically asked about sex but, given the chance to give feedback to an adult stranger who seemed interested, they didn't hesitate to write freely about sexual attitudes and behaviour amongst their peers. The final report was published as: *The Hothouse Society: An Exploration of Boarding-School Life Through the Boys' and Girls' Own Writing.* (Pelican, 1974.)

From about twelve years of age, pairing up into heterosexual couples was common amongst the boarders, usually a senior boy and a younger girl. Some senior boys reached down to the first year, to find themselves an eleven-year-old. We disapproved, but such a wide age gap was ignored by staff. Relationships often began at the Friday night dancing class or the Saturday night film, two places where we mixed across age groups. All the boarders had to attend dancing lessons, given by a professional teacher who wore a dance skirt with leggings and tapped a cane, as if she taught girls in a Parisian ballet school instead of lumpen teenagers at a Scottish boarding school. We learned the waltz, quickstep and foxtrot, in the hope that we would not disgrace ourselves in an imaginary future of dances and balls. The boys wore kilts and white gloves, the girls their best dresses. No one took the dancing seriously and every week Miss M's thread veins enlarged and reddened as her frustration rose. She was a screamer too.

At the start of the lesson, Miss M would tap on the wooden floor of the school hall and remind the boys to behave with dignity as they approached the girls to request the next dance. On the actual signal, the boys ran at full speed across the hall, pushing each other aside, to grab their preferred partner. The usual girls were chosen first, unless they held back, ignoring the snatching and tugging, because they were waiting for a certain boy to amble across. He didn't need to hurry, confident the girl knew that she was 'taken'. For days beforehand, she would have been prepared through verbal hints and written messages that he wanted to 'go' with her. She would make certain he knew that she had agreed. Once booked, she would not change partners between dances and he would walk her home, taking a detour around the back of the church hall and through the graveyard to Fairview.

There were rules about sex, established and followed by the pupils over generations; the boys would feel the girl's breasts under her bra and try to get their hands into her pants to rummage around her genitals. The girls wouldn't touch the boys at all except to kiss them, although it was always obvious when they were aroused. Intercourse was impossible because we simply couldn't get condoms. If a boy kept condoms in his locker, they would soon have been found by a matron and an uncomfortable conversation with a prefect, or the housemaster, would follow. Anything bought from the local chemist was on a 'chit', meaning that parents were sent an itemised invoice at the end of each term. The only option was to ask a day boy to buy condoms, but this was risky since the school leaked gossip like a wet dishcloth.

No matter how intensely a boy had been pursued by a girl, or vice-versa, pairing up was always unsatisfactory. School culture expected that once coupledom had been declared, you should spend all your time together, which meant missing all the group intrigue. The other reason for dissatisfaction was that neither the boys nor the girls had any idea how to give each other sexual pleasure. The boys didn't show the girls what they enjoyed, and they had no idea that touching a girl was meant for her satisfaction.

When boys and girls shared so much of their free time, particularly in the absence of parental oversight, it was natural for genuine relationships to form. The intense private feelings the boys expressed to their girlfriends were genuine and heartfelt, but their boarding house culture expected them to brag about their sexual success. The need to show off trumped loving feelings and inevitably led to rumours spreading about the girlfriend, followed by her being called a slag or a tart by other boys. This shaming left the girls suspicious and inhibited. The well-known problem of sexual bullying in all-male public schools had shifted intact to co-ed boarding, resulting in frustration, boredom and the loss of any possibility of shared sexual pleasure for both. If girls were believed to be the answer to boy-on-boy sexual exploitation, it was replaced by boy-on-girl sexual exploitation and the girls suffered.

The worst example of exploitation I heard about happened when a male boarding house set up a competition, the winning boy being the quickest to succeed in getting his hands into a girl's knickers. To be clear, the day girls were not included, this was aimed at girl boarders. The rules were as follows: set up a date, meet the challenge, abandon the girl and run back to the boarding house where a judge had to be persuaded of the 'evidence', in other words, by smelling the competitor's fingers. A boy from this boarding house told me about the competition the next day, and I was expected to find it funny. He assumed I would share his misogyny. I was furious, but at the same time felt a deep shame about my female body and its odours. The culprits were caught because a prefect in the boys' house overheard some of the talk and reported them. They were punished with gating but there was no public dressing down. The deep, underpinning problem of lack of respect for girl boarders was never addressed.

Things are worse now for girls, because of easily available pornography and the views of social influencers on the beliefs and expectations of adolescent boys. There was, and still is, a unique vulnerability for girl boarders educated amongst boys, living without the 'holding in mind' of responsible parents or without adequate supervision by adults. On 25 March 2021, journalist Olivia Petter wrote in *The Independent* newspaper about her own experience of boarding school culture, where older male students called new girls 'fresh meat', loudly assigning them numbers on a scale from one to ten according to their perceived attractiveness. The girls' trousers were pulled down in the dining hall while they were holding a tray, which meant they couldn't easily be pulled back up. Olivia recollects an experience close to my own, but almost fifty years apart:

> 'Things got worse when everyone started having sex. The girls were given nicknames based on how they behaved in bed while nude photographs of them were shared around campus. In the boys' boarding houses, sex with a woman was a prize. There were diagrams illustrating who had slept with whom and detailing exactly what they'd done and sixth formers would sometimes return from intimate encounters and stick their fingers in the younger boys' mouths. Those who'd had sex would readily brag about it and be literally applauded when they walked into a room.'

*

My first boyfriend, called Stinky by his friends, was about two years older than me. I was twelve, wore a vest and had not started my periods. On our first walk back to the boarding house, after the Saturday night film, he took my hand and we separated from our friends, striding past the boys' boarding houses, across a bridge, and followed the burn to the point where I knew we would turn off and go behind the church hall. My hand felt warm, tucked inside his and my stomach tightened with the excitement of a possible kiss. At last, I would know for myself how it felt to be under that boardwalk.

We stopped at the door to the church hall and Stinky broke in with ease. The dark, cavernous space smelt of dust and school dinners, the only light falling from high, arched windows. We tripped over benches and stacks of chairs until he dragged down a single chair with a crash and pulled me onto his knee, kissing me with wet lips that tasted of his boarding house tea. I felt his hands lift my skirt, there was a brush of fingers in my pants, and it was over. Time was short and we hurried back to Fairview where I stood amongst my form as they buttered bread and poured hot milk for cocoa, feeling unsure about what had happened and wishing I was one of them and not me.

The next day was Sunday and, keeping to tradition, Stinky met me at Fairview and we walked towards a woodland path that ran alongside a river south of the village. He asked whether I had talked to anyone about what we did the night before and when I said I hadn't, he named a senior girl he thought might be helpful. Whether he was afraid I might report him to a member of staff, or he was trying to be caring, I wasn't sure. He had no idea how little the girls shared about sex or anything else, unlike the boys. I agreed to speak to the older girl but knew I would not.

We pushed our way along the riverside through overgrown branches, searching for a private clearing amongst the trees, where we could lie down on our school coats and do whatever came next. I understood that my role was to be a passive recipient, acting only to stop him 'going too far', whatever that was. I felt little excitement, only worry that it might be hard to negotiate this unwelcome role as monitor of this boardwalk stuff.

We came upon a tent in the woods, with two of his friends waiting outside. Stinky feigned surprise, and the three of them smoked a cigarette, chatting as if their meeting was pure coincidence, then he raised the tent flap for me to go inside. The friends gave no sign of leaving and I could hear their murmured voices outside when we lay on the rubbery groundsheet. I allowed Stinky to kiss me but pushed his hand away from my flat chest. We walked back to Fairview in silence, his two friends trailing behind. The friendship, if it could even be called that, ended the next day. It was a hollow experience for us both, and while I might have been curious to discover more about sex, I wasn't willing to be used as a peep show for voyeurs. Besides, I had discovered his nickname was not an exaggeration, a surprise given how competitive the matrons were about hygiene. While Stinky may have smelt, I was lucky in one respect – he didn't brag about me to other boys.

It was almost a year before I was asked out again. My first serious boyfriend happened in fourth year, with a young man who is the focus of the chapter on sexual bullying and coercive control. His reputation, fuelled by his own propaganda, was that his girlfriends were enthusiastic about sex but only with him. This wasn't the reality of our friendship, during the few weeks of the summer term we spent together. On afternoons and long, summer evenings, in one of the secret, hidden places shared by school lovers, nothing more happened than the unplanned fumbling of our first encounter. In my diary, I wrote, 'I'm beginning to not enjoy going out at all.'

Being the girlfriend of this young adult was the beginning of my reputation as a 'tart'. I was sensitive to slights and it's likely the boys found this an easy way to provoke a reaction, but the name-calling wasn't in my imagination. I was called a tart often, by boys I hardly knew, for the remainder of my time in school. On a bus trip to the Glasgow Citizens Theatre in my sixth form, I sat next to my boyfriend, Neville. A boy seated in front of us turned around, his face twisted with self-righteous anger and shouted 'whore' into my face. Neville turned towards me and shrugged. He'd heard the taunts before, he said, had even wondered if they were true and wasn't going to challenge them.

I didn't want to be called a tart, or a whore, but I did want to have a boyfriend. As a solution, I came up with the kind of rigid and unhelpful strategy that children do, when they have to self-parent. In fifth year I decided to concentrate on my exams and avoid having a boyfriend at all, until the exams were over, and there would be no sex. By banning all sex, I reasoned, I could be sure any rumours spreading about me were untrue. The source of the gossip would be obvious, and I would immediately end the friendship.

Harry had slightly prominent teeth and ears, within a round, cheerful face. He excelled at seeking out news and gossip and was bright, especially with maths, but hid this well, hanging around with boys who had time to waste. He was a regular of the cafe crowd, a smoker and, more often than was wise, a drinker.

At dancing, Harry made me his regular partner. He chose me because we chatted easily but also because dancing with the same partner every week made a difference to our performance. We would not have admitted this to anyone else, but we liked mastering the dances and winning awards.

By the middle of the summer term, with the Scottish Highers over, Harry asked me to be his girlfriend. I wasn't keen and refused. The next day he tried a different strategy, one that was guaranteed to work with an anxious and insecure girl, telling me that some of the boys in our group didn't want me around anymore and many others in the school had a low opinion of me. Anyone with self-confidence would have been able to walk away but once my anxiety had been stoked, the safest option, for a person so obviously disliked and friendless, was to attach myself to my gaslighting friend. Harry was a skilled manipulator and by mid-May I wrote, without enthusiasm, 'Think I'm going with him.' He made the mistake of telling me that other boys had said I would be 'easy'. My decision about sex made sense; if people thought I was easy, including Harry, there would be none.

I was quickly bored with the tedious monotony of being a couple, but summer evening walks through woods scented with wild garlic, with some romantic handholding, softened me. I became fond of Harry, although I still insisted on the no-sex rule. I wrote, breathlessly, 'It's amazing we can have such a terrific relationship with no sex at all – it's fantastic. We're absolutely honest with each other. It's worked out so well really.' I'm not sure that Harry would have agreed.

Once Harry left school, we managed to meet in the summer holidays, since he was working in London and my family had moved to Northampton. My mother didn't like him, saying he was 'mean', not in the American sense of being nasty, which he certainly could be, but tight with money, which he wasn't. When we met, either in London or at my home, his mood often seemed low. I didn't have much free time since I worked long hours in my holiday job at Marks and Spencer, and it frustrated him that I couldn't be immediately available to fit in with his plans. On one of our long, dreary days wandering around Northampton, since my bedroom was off-limits, Harry seemed even more discontented and said that he wanted a 'cold, callous, experience'. I knew what he meant, and it wasn't on offer, at least not from me. From a fifty-year perspective, I can guess that Harry was asking for sex but not of the cold, callous sort he thought he wanted. He needed loving sex, with comfort and talking afterwards. Our friendship became testy, and Harry fell back on trying to control me by repeating cruel things other boys had said. I'd had enough of being manipulated and ended our relationship.

Harry had known exactly where my weaknesses lay, using this to control me, but I was playing a long, revenge-shaped game of my own. As an adolescent with an insecure-ambivalent relationship style, I was capable of demanding closeness while feeling a deep and hidden anger. This wasn't fair either; I should have explained how I felt about my reputation as a tart, encouraged him to apologise for his manipulation, and stuck to my refusal to be his girlfriend. It was a long time before I achieved enough insight to recognise this destructive dynamic in relationships and walk away from the unhealthy attraction of being manipulated, combined with the satisfaction of passive revenge. Although we met again, we never got the chance to put things right. Harry died well before his time, but I hope he grew up to respect women and find the love he was looking for.

On the surface, my adolescent relationships were no different from those of other generations. We were trapped within the well-worn story of girls seeking romance and boys wanting sex but in the absence of either adult guidance or parental control, both boys and girl boarders were fuelled by suspicion and resentment. By the time I was fifteen or sixteen, I understood that the boys' betrayal of the girls was the one insurmountable barrier we faced to enjoying a mutually satisfactory sexual experience. My parents had a copy of *The Joy of Sex* hidden in their bedroom, which I stole to read in my own room, always careful to return it to my mother's bedside drawer. Apart from surprise at the detailed drawings of where the bearded man was willing to put his face, the message was clear. Sex was meant to be enjoyed by men and women.

Our boyfriends would not have known, understood or cared that their sexual shaming of isolated young women was harmful to the girl's immediate sense of themselves as confident, sexual beings and if that shaming persisted for years, as it did with me, the effects would last a lifetime. The adults in charge of us should have known, understood and recognised their responsibilities but this did not happen.

CHAPTER 9

Sexual Bullying and Coercive Control

In my fourth year, I met a boy I will name Fisherman. This was not a nickname used at school, but his behaviour reminds me of the way a fly fisherman attracts his prey with an artificial lure, manipulates the catch at the end of a long line and hauls the fish in with a net. A fish can be landed without a fisherman ever using his hands, except to control the rod.

Most pupils boarded from the beginning of their Scottish secondary education, which meant they were eleven, going on twelve. Fisherman had started at eight, one of the youngest boarders ever and therefore more at risk than most of the long-term, destructive impact of a broken attachment from his family. He was rumoured to have been a pretty child, favoured by the matrons. When I met him, he was eighteen and in the sixth form but spent most of his time with younger pupils, including Oliver and Harry. Fisherman's choice of younger friends was a warning sign, but the younger boys were flattered by his attention and keen for his approval.

Although we had only the briefest acquaintance, he decided to lead a 'purge' against me. A purge is a campaign, favoured by former Soviet bloc countries, to rid society of people who don't fit. A purge at our school involved ignoring and silent treatment, name-calling and being left out – in other words, bullying. Since I had been bullied before, I recognised it immediately, and struggled to understand why I had become unpopular with older boys I hardly knew.

Our knowledge of attachment theory and bullying says that bullies tend to have higher scores on avoidant-attachment scales, whereas victims of bullying show higher levels of insecure-ambivalent attachment styles. Fisherman and I stepped comfortably into our predetermined roles when he decided to start bullying me. I have no idea why I caught his attention, but it may have been due to some imagined slight of Oliver, who felt I had abandoned him. Since I had widened my friendship group, I no longer showed much interest in Oliver and he may have believed, encouraged by Fisherman, that he had been unfairly cast aside. In his resentment, he developed a deep, simmering rage towards me, echoing his anger at his mother for her abandonment. The boy boarders thought they wanted sex from the girl boarders but their deepest need was for affection, parenting and friendship, needs that the girl boarders were unable to meet.

The bullying started with older boys and spread down to my year group; in class my chair was kicked from behind, and groups of boys followed me as I walked back to the boarding house, taunting me with names. One of the worst aspects of bullying today is that cyberbullying can creep into every second of a child's life and I was grateful the Fairview girls spared me that. The boys were more enthusiastic participants in Fisherman's purge than the girls, although some girls did seem less friendly towards me.

A repeat episode of bullying is always worse than the first, because it is so familiar. The loneliness, the shame and the fear of what might happen next haunted me but I had no idea how to seek help. Telling a member of staff wasn't an option, and even when my English teacher held me back one afternoon and asked if all was well, I couldn't say anything because his son was one of the tormentors. My parents couldn't be told because of their disappointment. I had allowed this to happen again, even after all the money spent on my education.

The purge affected me deeply. By the end of the first term of fourth year I wrote in my diary: 'The campaign had Fisherman and Oliver behind it. They managed to turn almost the whole school against me. Fisherman now tells me they succeeded. Everybody hated me. I have never been more miserable in my life. No wonder I did so badly in exams and had to take the rap for it at home.'

After the Christmas holidays, although the worst of the bullying was over, I still received threats. Harry enjoyed his role of active bystander, practising his coercion skills by warning me that, 'Something was going to happen, which would involve both him and Fisherman, and I wouldn't get any warning.' I was being threatened and should have been able to report this, but there was no one I could trust. In my diary I wrote the five words that haunts every bullied young person, every day: 'I'm so worried. Why me?' There had to be something wrong with me to be targeted again, and if the purge was discovered, I felt no confidence that adults would deal with the situation in a positive way. In fact, there was every likelihood my parents would be informed, I would be removed from the school and the matter considered closed, just as we had witnessed with Iona.

Of course, nothing happened except my anxiety increased. Harry's threat was empty because it was only the fear that mattered. A month later, he threatened me again, acting as Fisherman's mouthpiece, warning me that Fisherman was going to be 'nasty' because of my behaviour in the boarding house. At school, nothing was secret and there were few loyalties, so it is likely that a 'friend' from Fairview informed Fisherman of something I had done or said, which he used to justify further punishment. Again, nothing actually happened, it was all about control, but the anxiety stayed with me every day and through each night.

Later in the month, on a Sunday, I was passed a note from Oliver, asking me to meet him in the club that afternoon. We talked all afternoon, heads bowed together in the low light of the games room, which had once been an infants' classroom, with arched windows set high on the walls and wooden panelling. We reminisced about our shared past, laughing about our junior teacher throwing Lesley out of the classroom whenever her taunts went too far. Oliver reassured me that the purge was over, and on cue, Fisherman arrived. I immediately felt afraid but he greeted me like an old friend, a powerful but benevolent figure who had the power to harm me but also to rescue me.

The reason for their manipulation became apparent in the next few days. The threats were a device to create fear, the meeting in the club designed to soothe, so that I would gratefully accept another invite to meet Oliver. The Teapot cafe in February was gloomy and dank, but we sometimes preferred the Teapot to Tangs, mainly because it was cheaper. On a Monday evening, left alone by the group, Oliver traced the sticky table top with his fingers, unable to look at me. I pressed him to tell me what was wrong, my antennae throbbing with the risk of another threat. Oliver lifted his eyes and asked me to be his girlfriend. I refused.

At school the next day, Oliver threatened me with a further purge. This turned out to be nothing more serious than being ignored by him, which was no loss, but the fear meant I stayed trapped within their control.

While Fisherman, Harry and Oliver had been the main instigators, and had the power to decide when to end the official bullying, many other boys had heard about the purge or participated in some way. These boys felt entitled to subject me to cruel comments for months to come, a constant reminder that I remained vulnerable to further bullying. In the end, I wasn't the only victim. Oliver learned the hard lesson that being associated with Fisherman, who was powerful but not liked or respected, forever changed how he was regarded by other pupils. Once Oliver no longer had Fisherman's protection, he became an isolated and lonely figure.

While Fisherman had called off his purge, he wasn't finished with me. One Saturday night in March, watching *Cat Ballou* in the school hall, the teacher in charge stopped the projector to change the reel. As the lights went on and the buzz of conversation rose, I was passed a message. It was hard to read at first, my eyes squinting in the sudden brightness, but I had been asked to meet the almost-man who held enough power to turn everyone against me. He was waiting for me in the foyer at the bottom of the stairs leading up to the hall, his boyish face showing his characteristic, lop-sided grin.

Leaning against the wall, hands in pockets, Fisherman's verbal assault on my personality took up the entire second half of the film. I heard myself described as someone who led others on. I used people, then threw them aside. I wasn't to be trusted. As soon as the film ended and chairs rumbled above us, Fisherman disappeared. Fairview girls crowded around me in the foyer and asked where I'd been, but I couldn't speak. What if it was true? What if I told them and they agreed with what he'd said?

Telling another person how they should think or behave, without this being requested, is a sign of limited emotional maturity in the advice-giver but if the recipient is anxious, with poorly developed emotional resilience, such controlling behaviour can be confused with genuine concern. The other person might be critical, but at least they have thought about you, they hold you in mind, so they must care. If the message is a cruel one, you probably deserve it. For a young adolescent, starved of such attention, Fisherman's words carried great power.

Characteristic of coercive control, the hidden purpose of his 'advice' was to increase his power over me.

Afterwards, at the club, I stood with other Fairview girls and chatted to Fisherman and his young friends as if nothing had happened, trying to hear what was being said above the pounding rock music. Once I was alone, I admitted only to my diary that I was scared of him. 'He'll leave me friendless again, he'll spread the word that I'm someone who picks up friends and then throws them aside.'

Only a few days later, at dancing, Harry passed me another message from Fisherman, instructing me to meet him at the village cafe the following afternoon. I believed I had no choice. The gap in our ages and seniority in the school was enough of a power imbalance, never mind my lack of confidence following his analysis of my worthless character and the fear of more bullying. We met in the Teapot. Unusually, the jukebox was pounding out the words of 'Young Girl' by Gary Puckett and the Union Gap. It was hard to talk, so Fisherman said we should go for a walk.

We ended up at the track of the former railway, hidden from sight, and Fisherman pulled me towards him by my coat, kissing me, then moving his hands under my blouse and into my knickers. It was too fast and too sudden, but how could I say no and still be the kind of person who didn't 'lead others along'? He was already an adult, one who had the power to turn people against me. Given the control he had over me through his bullying and gaslighting, there was no question of legitimate consent. Sex is always abusive, if initiated by a more powerful figure upon a victim who feels he or she must cooperate because they have no choice. Those skilled at coercive control can manipulate through a spectrum of behaviour, from actual force and open threats to subtle persuasion.

There was no gentlemanly walk home either. I trudged back to Fairview, unescorted. Beyond my immediate shame and disbelief, there were two pressing worries: had we been seen and how long would it be before he bragged to other boys? I gave no thought to the fact that Fisherman was meant to be the boyfriend of another Fairview girl. Although I could name emotions and recognise them in everyone but myself, my limited emotional development had stopped on the day I entered boarding school. I did not yet have the ability to walk in another person's emotional shoes. In the boarding house, I revealed nothing to his girlfriend and tried to stop anyone else from telling her I'd been with Fisherman, without revealing anything about what had happened.

By the following day, she knew, but I didn't apologise. Later that afternoon, Fisherman added to her humiliation by passing her a message, to give to me, with a time and place where we must meet. For anyone who has not been in a coercive relationship, my behaviour is a puzzle. Wasn't I a girl who cared desperately about friendships and whether other people liked me, a girl who worried about her reputation? Yet I thought had no choice but to allow the same thing to happen again.

Fifty years ago, we hadn't heard about coercive control but adolescent girls in the present day, some as young as fourteen, have experience of coercively controlling behaviour from boyfriends, and feel every bit as trapped as I did. These young girls report that being isolated, controlled and diminished as individuals leaves them feeling powerless and they fear repercussions if they try to escape from the relationship. Some feel worried that their parents and other adults will not take their concerns seriously and other girls reject help, preferring to manage in their own way. Little has changed.

The Women and Equalities Committee Report: Attitudes Towards Women and Girls in Education Settings, UK Parliament, 2016, reported that:

- Almost a third (29%) of 16–18-year-old girls say they have experienced unwanted sexual touching at school.

- Nearly three-quarters (71%) of all 16–18-year-old boys and girls say they hear terms such as 'slut' or 'slag' used towards girls at schools on a regular basis.

- 59% of girls and young women aged 13–21 said in 2016 that they had faced some form of sexual harassment at school or college in the past year.

The government's follow-up investigation in 2023 reported that:

> 'Our work on violence against women and girls, and that of our predecessor Committee, consistently found that men and boys were overwhelmingly the

> main perpetrators of sexual harassment and sexual violence. We have also examined the attitudes that perpetuated gender-based violence, such as male ideas around gender, what it was to be a man, and masculinity. Several contributors to this inquiry noted the prevalence of misogynistic attitudes—rooted in myths about rape and violence against women—that have allowed men and boys to get away with sexual harassment and sexual violence, invalidated women's and girls' experiences, and inhibited disclosure.'

Misogyny towards girls and women continues to be at the heart of school culture, just as it was in the 1960s, but educators and psychologists now know that the most vulnerable boys are drawn towards such views and behaviour through the security and group cohesion that follows from holding shared beliefs. This is an important lesson for those who care for young boy boarders, a group now recognised as vulnerable and at risk of emotional harm. These unparented boys will require active teaching and modelling of mutual, respectful relationships with girls and women and nurturing, supportive interventions from male role models in their prep schools, to counteract the power of misogynist beliefs.

*

Fisherman asked me to be his girlfriend and I found the confidence to refuse. A rejection wasn't part of his plan, so he had to hurt me back. Salacious details about me and his former girlfriend circulated, including a taunt that

'Anyone could have had me that weekend.' It is obvious that Fisherman was trying to manipulate me and hurt his girlfriend at the same time, but we didn't talk about it, or try to protect each other, even though we had known each other for years. This was the reality of our life in Fairview. Survival was a solitary business.

Fisherman continued his attempts to control both of us, one day waiting for me outside school to tell me that he had spent hours with the Boss. Expulsion from school was a possibility and it was going to be 'nasty', he said, for both his ex-girlfriend and me. Truth was always a permeable boundary for Fisherman, but he never wasted an opportunity to use fear to manipulate another person, particularly a girl. Seeing my shock, the threat was quickly retracted, but I had to live through a few anxious days until I felt confident we weren't involved. I never did learn what he had done to put his school place at risk. It would have been entirely proper if his bragging about his sexual conquests had been reported and taken seriously by an adult, but this was unlikely.

Train journeys were the bookends of every term for those of us whose homes were far from the school. The trains still had compartments, with sagging seats, mesh luggage racks and faded upholstery smelling of dust. Since many of us travelled, it was possible to be confined in a compartment for hours with someone you would not have chosen. At the end of the spring term, my sister and I found ourselves trapped with Fisherman and another boy from her year. There was a dining car, where it was possible to escape for hours, with afternoon tea served from heavy teapots that always dripped onto the starched, white tablecloth. Peggy and her friend went to the dining car, and I was left alone with Fisherman. Again and again he tried to persuade, cajole and manipulate me to go with him into one of the toilet cubicles, but I wasn't going to be caught out a third time. I trusted that he wouldn't manhandle me into a toilet but he could physically prevent me leaving the compartment, since he had positioned himself at the door, with his legs stretched across as a barrier. Instead, I stared out of the window or tried to read, but he kept up his barrage of sexual bullying for hours, his eyes never leaving my face, only stopping when our companions returned.

Like women and girls from the beginning of time, the only real control I had over Fisherman was to keep him close. Resisting him meant facing the threat of another purge, to never feel free or safe to walk the streets of our village or join friends in the cafe or the club. Until he left school, Fisherman would always be present, threatening, criticising or manipulating. The coerced will agree to anything if this prevents other behaviours that are even more worrying or frightening.

When he asked me again to be his girlfriend, at the beginning of the summer term, I agreed. It would only be for a few months, I reasoned. The fear of being bullied was removed but replaced by a raft of new worries; would I be able to control the sex and what would other people say about me?

For the rest of the summer term, I tried to be vigilant. 'It's going to be difficult, all this holding out.' When a weekend party was arranged in Glasgow, I made sure I couldn't attend, knowing I would be pressurised to sleep with him. He was unfaithful at the party, of course, and told me. I tried to use this to end our relationship, but he first became angry and then sorry and affectionate. Sharing of emotion was risky for Fisherman, and he avoided me for a day or two afterwards. When we met, he told me that 'everyone', including all the teachers and the Boss, thought it was a good thing we were going out together. This wasn't true but, desperate for approval, I didn't challenge him for evidence and swallowed the lie.

We met every evening and at weekends, as school culture expected. I was flattered when Fisherman told me his life story, the sad details of his unloved childhood, but he never enquired about mine. The age difference and my lack of commitment meant that I was often bored and as I grew in confidence, I became teasing, silly and difficult. The days ticked by towards the end of term, when he would leave school forever, and we struggled to manage our differing insecurities. I overshared my worries about the coming year, and he risked revealing his sadness at leaving. We settled into a pattern of becoming nasty, making up, and being nasty again.

At the end of term, my family left immediately for a holiday in Wales and on my return, there were two letters from Fisherman questioning my silence, even though we had only been apart for a week. My mother fell ill that summer and had to be hospitalised for the majority of her break from school. My father was working, my sister Peggy had a summer job before starting university and I was left to run the household: cleaning, shopping, cooking for the family and entertaining my younger brother, Alex. Without my daily presence and enough written contact, Fisherman struggled with his conflicting emotions and he seesawed between critical, threatening letters and others that were reasonable and friendly. I barely missed him and did not pretend otherwise. In August, he finished things between us, telling me his new girlfriend owned a dog called Isobel.

Intermittent contact continued between us until 1971, despite the end of our relationship, ricocheting between cruelty, warnings, kindness and gifts. Although Fisherman was a university student, who should have been looking forward to an exciting life with new friends, he still tried to control boys at school about their attitudes and behaviour towards me.

This attachment 'dance', played out between us, reveals how an insecure attachment profile can last into adult life, unless actively addressed. For Fisherman, genuine feelings of attachment were so unfamiliar and uncomfortable that he had to be cruel and controlling, even reaching back from his adult life to manipulate former school friends.

I was the perfect target. Easily upset by worries about belonging and being liked, the more dismissive or unkind his behaviour was, the more I needed to keep him close. When he allowed himself to be vulnerable and share his true feelings with me, I harmed him by being inconsistent and unresponsive, repeating behaviour only too familiar from his childhood.

In adulthood, it is common for people with an insecure attachment profile to become friends or lovers, since adults who have grown up with a secure attachment profile tend to prefer each other. When both have an anxious-avoidant attachment profile, they may rub along quite well if neither asks for much support or kindness, as long as there are no children. A couple who both have an anxious-ambivalent attachment style may share a relationship that is turbulent and full of drama, which they both enjoy, but can be equally harmful for children. The most damaging relationship is one where an individual with an anxious-ambivalent profile partners someone with an anxious-avoidant profile. This couple will forever be engaged in chasing and running away from each other, with one partner ratcheting up the emotional temperature and the other becoming increasingly distant, dismissive and controlling. Children raised by emotionally vulnerable and insecure adults will always replicate their own parents' mistakes, both in childhood and adulthood. It is possible for adults to change, however, with insight gained through reading or perhaps counselling, and by making a conscious choice to behave differently towards others and any children they are raising.

Children who live at home with their parents at least have a chance of being protected from harmful relationships, particularly if adults watch, listen and are willing to set rules, including limiting and monitoring the child's use of social media. I could not have shared my fears about Fisherman with my parents, but had they known about him, they would have forbidden me to see him. Our carers at school, however, turned a blind eye. For a child of fourteen, without help from adults, the bullying and my subsequent relationship with Fisherman was an intolerable situation, one which felt impossible to manage on my own.

Within the population of boys at school, Fisherman was not typical. Most boys held misogynistic views and their attitudes towards women and girls were typical of their generation but they were not usually predatory or very interested in being controlling. Fisherman's problems were complex and unique and it was unfortunate that our paths crossed. Other girls must have been his victims, with long-term consequences similar to mine, but I never learned who they were.

Having been Fisherman's girlfriend, I was labelled as a tart and the boy boarders felt entitled to taunt me with this jibe until I left school. Even in my sixth form, my brother told me he had overheard senior boys in his boarding house referring to me as a 'whore' and an 'ugly bitch'. I wasn't a whore, nor was I ugly, but I admit that sometimes I could be a bitch. Facing almost daily taunts simply for being female, a girl who was already struggling with the complexities and pitfalls of our archaic rules about sexual behaviour, affected my relationships at school and into the future.

CHAPTER 10

The Staff

School staff came in two broad types, those who had been at the school forever and held traditional values about behaviour, and a younger group influenced by the popular culture of the late 1960s, who were inclined to challenge the old order when it suited them. Most teachers were given a nickname but a few never were. With hindsight, those teachers were the most respected.

Our teachers rarely had problems with discipline in lessons, since class sizes were small and the pupils motivated. If we started chatting or staring out of the window, we were frequently reminded that we were wasting our parents' money. One member of the modern languages staff had our fees worked out by the minute and if we wasted time, he would look at his watch and chalk up the debt we owed our parents on the blackboard. Male and female teachers had separate staffrooms, the men's room called the Male Staff Correction Room, which meant their 'marking' room, but could be interpreted in other ways. Children sent to the men's staffroom at break risked being choked in a cloud of smoke through the open door. This was not true of the women's staffroom.

If there had been a more interesting conversation in the staffroom during break, teachers felt comfortable to sweep into the classroom ten minutes late, carrying with them the smell of cigarettes on their gowns and coffee on their breath, absolutely confident that the class would not be in uproar.

Our teachers who dealt with facts, experiments and languages tended to be less chatty than those who taught us about poetry, art and world affairs. These creative types seemed able to tolerate animated behaviour, shouting out and laughing, without the fear of losing control. Our relationship with all staff improved as we became more senior in the school, and with familiarity came indiscretion. In my diary I recorded a conversation with my history teacher who was leaving, just before our Higher exams. 'He's so upset – that's why he's leaving. The teachers can't communicate with us anymore. We're dull, lifeless, never have fun. We've had it all beaten out of us.' Our new history teacher started in January and wasted no time in dismissing the skills of his predecessor.

Mr D was one of the members of staff without a nickname, a newly qualified teacher who took the considerable risk of starting the club. He was approachable and open to listening to pupils, although this wasn't my personal experience of him. There were only two occasions in my seven years at school when a member of staff asked about me personally. Once was during the bullying episode, or purge, when my English teacher asked why I didn't smile anymore. The second time was in the sixth form, when the Boss questioned me about a relationship break-up, which was terrifying. Mr D respected me and my ability in English, but I don't think he liked me, in part because I joined in with teacher-baiting and arguing. On balance, I would have preferred to be liked.

Another teacher I hoped would like me was our art teacher, who we called by his first name rather than a nickname. He was a respected artist and he ran a relaxed studio, full of music and light, on the top floor of the school. I believed I was one of the best artists in the class and wondered why he gave me so little praise. He was also discouraging whenever I mentioned the possibility of art college. We were expected to maintain a sketchbook and I was diligent about mine, which meant that he always chose several of my sketches to hang in the yearly exhibition for parents. In June of fourth year I wrote: 'B said he hoped I'd passed my O level.' I was hurt by such faint praise, but now I recognise that my paintings lacked the creativity I saw in other pupils' work, even those who were less technically competent than I was. He probably didn't much like the work he chose from my sketchbooks but thought my skilled draughtsmanship would impress the parents. I think I annoyed him, and he believed I wasn't serious, because art was where I met Steven. We always sat together, and inevitably talked and laughed too much.

As a child desperate to be liked, whenever the opportunity arose, my focus would be on relationships rather than work. In the classroom, children like me, with relationship anxiety, can be attention-seeking and demanding. I wasn't always a nuisance, however. If I found the work easy, I was able to gain enough adult attention by doing well. In subjects where I struggled, those where the teachers enforced strict rules, my behaviour was rarely a concern because I was so afraid of their anger. The one subject where my attitude caused real problems was maths. By fourth year, I was in the lowest set and kept the same teacher throughout the Higher course, a relaxed man who tolerated a great deal of teasing and answering back from pupils. This combination of low discipline and high subject anxiety resulted in me showing off with annoying 'class clown' behaviour. I was fully aware of how my acting-out was being received but I simply couldn't control myself.

Our teachers didn't go in for praise, but this was Scotland in the late 1960s, and perhaps, as Philip Larkin wrote about sex, praise was only discovered in 1963. Most of our parents didn't believe in praise either; the fear of a child becoming lazy or spoilt far outweighed any risk of their child losing confidence or giving up.

Criticism or fear is not usually effective as a motivator because the impact depends entirely upon the young person's previous background and experience. Some children will be motivated and try harder, others will ignore the comments, and a few children will decide it's not worth trying at all. Effective use of praise is nuanced; it has to be delivered with skill and, to be truly effective, must be specific and genuine. Some children have had such a difficult start with relationships, they cannot accept praise at all. The child believes they are worthless, so any praise must be a lie. These children require judicious use of praise from skilled, caring and observant teachers, since misjudgements can result in falsely praised work being destroyed by the child.

*

The tension between teachers who wanted life at school to stay the same, forever, and those who fought for change, came to a head in June 1970 when the sixth form wrote a 'manifesto' recommending a sixth form council instead of the prefect system. Prefects were in an unenviable situation, neither pupils nor staff, but expected to enforce rules and report other pupils for wrongdoing. This led to some complex dilemmas for individual prefects. As head girl, Peggy was asked by the housemistress of Fairview to question me about a girl in my form, whether she was having sex with her boyfriend. This was not a concern for the girl's well-being; the intention was to catch the girl out in a disciplinary matter. Luckily, my sister and I were close enough to recognise each other's predicament and we concocted a story that would provide enough detail to appear truthful but not incriminate the young couple.

A few days after the manifesto was circulated, the pupils held a vote on the proposal and the recommendation for a sixth form council was passed by the student body. We heard later that the staff were riven with disagreement and a furious teacher had destroyed our voting papers in front of his colleagues. The head of maths resigned from teaching his sixth form class and the Boss refused to meet with student representatives.

Towards the end of the month, a further staff meeting took place behind locked doors, with the caretaker on guard. The following day, we had a free afternoon for the annual staff golf match. I wrote in my diary that the golfing was unlikely to be convivial. On the morning of the match, the sixth form were finally called in to meet the Boss and were told that any discussion of a council would be deferred until the following year. The Boss recommended that the sixth form be made more exclusive through requiring four Highers for entry. This did not go down well, since the pupils' ambition had been to reduce privilege, not create another layer of entitlement. In the end, a threatened entry requirement into the sixth form was quietly forgotten, since there was no solution to the problem of fifth formers who hadn't passed four Highers. Parents already struggled to fork out more fees for an unnecessary sixth form. It was unlikely any would pay for a child to repeat fifth year.

The staff believed they had spoken, and the matter was settled. On the last full day of term, the names of the new prefects for the following year were read out at morning prayers. That night, an attack on the home of the head of maths seemed an inevitable outcome of the resentment felt by drunken members of the departing sixth form. They had tried for change but failed. That they got the wrong house was a tragedy for the elderly owner, who woke to find her house daubed in swastikas, but no doubt became a dining-out conversation for those involved, once time had erased their guilt.

*

To keep the club working there had to be an adult present, at least on a Saturday night, and that was usually Mr D with help from prefects. Mr D was an assistant housemaster and a single man. Those teachers who were actual housemasters or mistresses probably argued that they couldn't help, since they were unable to leave their boarding houses unattended, although this level of care didn't seem to stretch to the girls, left in sole charge of matrons at weekends. The rest of the staff, those with responsibilities limited to the classroom, offered no assistance.

Of course, boys often got drunk. I recorded in my diary that on the same night a group of boys were caught with alcohol, we played the 'F' song from Woodstock on repeat, leaping around and chanting along with the words, even though it was a forbidden track. We often trailed back late to our boarding houses, claiming that no adult had warned us about the time. It wasn't long before a self-important prefect reported the drinking to the Boss, going over Mr D's authority. I was furious. 'I realise that the club could be closed forever if they drink again but I believe that a pupil should never take these things on themselves.' The club limped on for a few more weeks but by the end of November it was closed until the beginning of the next term because of our apparent 'lack of cooperation'. I felt sorry for Mr D, who had tried hard on our behalf, but old-school staff had always believed the club was a bad thing. It must have been galling that they were proved right. Mr D changed his style, pretending to take on a tough, conservative approach but we weren't convinced and made fun of him. It is hardly surprising that Mr D soon decided he had no long-term future at our school but went on to have a highly successful career elsewhere.

We had a problem, my cohort, with taking things too far. Young people of previous generations had managed to tread a line between cooperation and rebellion or between humour and insult, which became lost by the late 1960s. The club was a godsend, saving senior pupils from hours of tedium in the boarding houses and allowing boarders to mix in a warm space at weekends without spending our parents' money in the cafes. Its failure showed our lack of imagination. We should have fought to protect it.

Another example was the leavers' show. For decades, final year pupils staged an end-of-year play for the whole school, where they were allowed free rein with the script. My memory of these is of well-rehearsed skits with caricatures of staff that may have been barely close to acceptability but were not cruel. By 1970, an unprecedented level of distrust had developed between staff and pupils and the writers had to submit the script for adult scrutiny. Of course, the leavers' show was scrapped that year and the tradition was never re-established. Our school newspaper, for years written and edited by pupils, went the same way.

CHAPTER 11

Women Adrift

Growing up in the 1960s, we were aware of having many great aunts, often spinsters and usually called something like Jean or Mary. They were teachers and shared houses in places like North Berwick. Middle-class women in Britain were disproportionately affected by the loss of officers in the First World War and, as a society, we have assumed that our great aunts were single by default rather than choice. But single women teachers were able to have a full working life, with pension rights established in 1918. Married women teachers were often forced to give up their posts, since the marriage bar was widely enforced. In schools where it was hard to fill a teaching position, married women were able to carry on working, but their jobs were not secure, they were never considered for promotion and they often faced the disapproval of their colleagues. The marriage bar for woman teachers lasted until the 1944 Education Act. Only the civil service offered the same pension benefits, but those jobs were mainly clerical, without any possibility of promotion. Our unmarried great aunts, who were teachers, may well have been a great deal more satisfied with their working life than history has suggested.

After the end of World War One, women without the qualifications or background to become teachers sought work in childcare, as nannies or boarding school matrons. Employment as a nanny brought a room and meals but the tiresome responsibility of caring for children all day and well into the evening. The boarding school matron benefitted from a room and food, as well as the luxury of long holidays without the boarders, often in an attractive house in a countryside setting. Schools more than families were likely to pay into a pension fund, so being a matron was a sought-after position.

For both nannies and matrons, wages would have been low, and these women must have found it impossible to save enough for a small bolthole after retirement, leaving them dependent for a home upon their own family. Those without parents or a married sister or brother may well have tried to work for years after it was sensible to do so, hiding their age from their employer.

I first met this deception when my mother's desperate need for childcare collided with another woman's desperate need for accommodation and wages. Janet was our live-in housekeeper, employed by my family after we moved from the farm in Northumberland to a village in Scotland. Janet had white hair and staring eyes, and to me, she looked older than my grandmother. We didn't see her at breakfast, but during the day she was expected to manage some light household tasks, although she was so frail and slow-moving it's possible she spent her days in an armchair, chain-smoking. Her duties in the evening were to give us tea after school, always chewy toast and a rock-hard boiled egg. She never spoke but gazed into space, drinking strong tea, with her fags and matches on the table. After tea, she supervised my brother's bath, making sure he was clean and in pyjamas when my mother arrived home from teacher training college in Dundee. After a brief exchange between the two women, Janet disappeared into her room, a place we were not allowed to visit. I don't think she had a television, even though I listened with my ear pressed to her door to catch the telltale theme tunes of familiar programmes.

Janet wasn't with us long before she became seriously ill and had to stay in her room. Days passed when she couldn't raise herself from her bed and a doctor had to be called. Janet had no safety net for her terminal cancer and had had no choice but to find work with accommodation, even after her diagnosis. The atmosphere in our home became tense, my mother often disappearing into Janet's room, tight-lipped, and carrying out a tray or a bedpan. If we asked how Janet was, we were shushed. In the end, my mother traced a relative and Janet vanished. We weren't told when she left, except that her bedroom door stood ajar, revealing a single bed with a neat candlewick bedspread. She died a few weeks later.

Within a year, I met Miss Kent, the matron of Rosehill. She seemed elderly, but all older women looked the same once their hair had faded and they wore glasses. I had no reason to suspect she would meet the same fate as Janet. The degree of her ill health only became clear when her breathing became fast and shallow if she hurried too quickly upstairs, and she wore a mask whenever a task involved fibres or dust, such as sorting towels or laundry. Miss Kent died unexpectedly, during the school holidays, and was never spoken of again, either at home or at school.

Janet and Miss Kent were unusual; they did not appear to openly dislike children. Janet was indifferent, but she may have been preoccupied with her own imminent death. Miss Kent was kind and gentle. The other 'Misses' I met, whether teachers or matrons, were in the wrong profession, burning with indignation and rage at the unfairness of their lives. I have no idea what that unfairness was. As the generation who followed after them, we smugly assumed they were angry because they hadn't found a man, but that is simplistic. We can only guess that their frustration, unfortunately directed at us, may have had more to do with hopes lost, ambitions failed and the grinding fear of poverty.

My last matron in Fairview, the one we called 'Nelly', did not completely fit the profile as she referred to herself as 'Mrs'. She deceived everyone about her age to snap up a job with a lovely room in our Scottish baronial boarding house. Once again, the desperation of the school to find a matron chimed with the despair of an impoverished woman. Nelly wore a wig, which often slipped, showing a few strands of greying hair on her bald scalp, she wore hearing aids and had a marked dowager's hump. We should have enjoyed Nelly's little dog, who came as an unarguable condition of her accepting the post, but he yapped constantly and bit our ankles as he snuffled across our beds at lights out, mistaking our feet for rabbits. Once the junior girls were in bed, Nelly had no energy to enforce any rules. Her sitting room door was closed, her TV turned up to the fullest volume, and she fell asleep. This suited us when all was well but Nelly was not safe to be in charge overnight, even with the support of an assistant matron who lived in the village. As deputy head of the girls in my sixth form, I had to step in when two girls became ill overnight. I believed they needed close monitoring but only when I shouted at her and demanded that she notice their symptoms, did Nelly finally take charge.

*

In my late teens, when I had left school and was existing in the hollow interregnum between school and university, I met another group of lost women. My home town, Northampton, had a private psychiatric hospital, with extensive grounds, almost in the centre of town. It was a hospital with a reputation for innovation and excellence, but its past as a Victorian asylum still haunted its polished corridors and high, stained-glass windows. My sister worked there during her university holidays and, as a medical student, was lauded as a higher being, with almost-nurse status on the wards. On the other hand, I was a school leaver without any redeeming characteristics and instead of meeting the director of nursing on my first day, I briefly met the housekeeper and was escorted to Women's Geriatric, a ward hiding in the turrets. I had no idea where I was or how to escape, a problem I shared with the residents. I was to be the ward orderly, I was told, but without any training or even a description of my duties.

The date was 1971, and the patients were in their eighties or nineties, which means they would have been born around 1890. The ward had its own small kitchen, which was where I waited, restless and embarrassed, until the matron found me. Had I had forgotten the residents' morning coffee and biscuits, she shouted, until, seeing my blank expression, she helped me lay out a trolley with cups and saucers, made a pot of instant coffee and showed me the familiar red tin of Peek Freans Family Circle assortment, hidden at the back of the cupboard next to the flowery plates.

Pushing the trolley, I followed matron to the day room, where the women ate at a long central table made of oak, circled by groups of faded armchairs under dormer windows. The shared common room, the rules and the routine, reminded me of the boarding school I had just left. I served the coffee, chatting to those who wanted to talk. Some of the patients stared at a point in the distance, lost in their own visions, others rocked back and forth, humming, or talking to someone unseen. But there were at least two women, dressed smartly in tweeds, with whiskery chins and broad smiles, who put down their newspapers and engaged me in sensible conversation. I noticed a stream of urine pool under one of the resident's chairs and hurried to tell the matron but was sharply reminded, with rolled eyes, that mopping up pee was one of my duties. I finished serving the coffee and chatted to the ladies before I cleaned up, and no one seemed to mind. Dealing with the ladies' piss and shit was not a priority on the ward, which accounted for the smell.

At lunchtime, I was joined in the kitchen by another orderly, an older woman who possibly had learning difficulties, or was I just being unkind? The ward lunch arrived through a hatch, its arrival announced by rumbling sounds from the pulley and a meaty smell. With my new companion, I set the table and we laid out the food, serving the ladies who were able to come to the table. The nurses disappeared with trays to rooms in corridors beyond the ward, places I never visited. Some of the patients ate in silence, chewing slowly with badly fitting false teeth, but once again, I observed at least two women attempt a sensible conversation. When one patient started to wail, one of the articulate pair asked her to be quiet, reminding the distressed woman in a voice redolent of her authority and class that she was ruining everyone's lunch.

The other orderly disappeared. After mopping more urine from the day room floor, I washed and dried the lunch plates in my little kitchen and wondered what to do next. I was hungry but had no idea when I could take a break or where the staff canteen was. Before she left, the other woman, the one with possible learning difficulties, said I should make the ladies an afternoon tea of jam sandwiches, so I found bread and a large tin of jam, cramming slices of Mother's Pride and margarine into my mouth as I worked. There was no such thing as cling wrap in 1971, and I couldn't find any greaseproof paper, so I sat alone, staring at the curling sandwiches, waiting to be found.

Matron was furious but luckily not with me. She demanded to know if I'd been given any training but didn't wait for an answer. With cold patience, she asked if I thought it wise to make bread sandwiches at two o'clock and not serve them until four. Who had told me to do that? I accused the woman who had helped earlier and listened to matron's rant about the neglect of their ward. Didn't she have enough to do without stupid girls and women with learning difficulties, who were no help at all? I could only nod in agreement as matron slammed the sandwiches into the waste bin. She made the residents fresh tea and instructed me to serve more biscuits.

By now, I had been on the ward for eight hours without a break, but I couldn't admit that I didn't know when I was expected to finish, or how to find my way back to the outside. This was a downside of my boarding school education. I had a veneer of confidence, so was rarely offered the help I needed, but had been left without the inner resources or confidence to ask for support. An hour later, the patients' dinner rumbled its way up the lift shaft and after I had helped to serve, the individual residents were led away to their rooms to begin the complicated nighttime routine of bathing, bed and medication. The matron found me washing up in the kitchen, tearful and exhausted. When I reluctantly confessed that I didn't know my way out, she rolled her eyes again, but led me down steep staircases and silent corridors, to a door that opened out onto the bright relief of a summer's evening.

I learned my role and survived for a week or two until the housekeeper moved me to another ward. The money was good, and I was intrigued by the residents. The work wasn't difficult, once I had established a routine, and I had plenty of time to talk to the patients, if they were able. The nurses would not discuss the residents' mental health with me, but I learned that several were titled, most were from the upper classes, and none had any visitors. When I asked if the more capable patients were ever taken outside, since even I knew that community care was beginning to be favoured over closed wards, the nurses answered that the outside world would only worry and frighten their patients. These ladies went nowhere but the ward. I dared to ask about one woman, who seemed entirely lucid, and was told she had been a patient for all of her adult life.

Some of the women I met may have been caught within the net of the Mental Deficiency Act of 1913, which even at the time, critics said would be used to regulate and control women. One diagnosis for which a woman could be committed to an asylum was that of 'moral imbecile', which meant the girl or woman had behaved outside society's expectations regarding her sexual behaviour. Any woman found having sex outside marriage, or falling pregnant, could be sent to an asylum by their family and never visited again. Without family support and determination, it was possible for a daughter or sister to remain in an asylum for the rest of her life. I cannot know for sure if any of the delightful and wholly sane ladies I met, living out the end of their lives in the eaves of St Andrew's Hospital, were victims of this act but I suspect this may have been the case. The act was repealed in 1959, by which time these elderly patients were institutionalised and forgotten.

One patient had her own room, and her imperious requests, shouted from within, were treated with grudging respect. On those few weeks I worked on the ward, every morning after breakfast she bellowed that all the 'darkies' should line up in her room. It was shocking to hear these words, ringing out with all the racism, privilege, and entitlement of her class, unmodified by any access to modern culture or society. Most of the nurses were women of colour and at matron's insistence, they reluctantly complied, already knowing what they would hear. One day I listened outside the open door. In a crisp, cut-glass accent, the patient announced that she had arranged a flight home for them all. If they stepped forward, she would give them their tickets. She was delusional, with little self-awareness or control and I was puzzled that the nurses cooperated with this daily humiliation. I was told she was a titled woman from the British aristocracy and by agreement, the nurses felt they had no choice but to play along with her commands. The closed world of this ward, with its rules and customs dominated by tradition and habit, was like boarding school, where the powerless conform to prevent worse harm to themselves but take out their revenge on those even less powerful. I witnessed this dynamic through small, subtle acts of bullying of the patients by staff, so endemic within the culture of the ward, it was not hidden from me. Our aged patients may not have had visitors but were occasionally sent flowers. In a not-so-subtle example of bullying, a nurse waved a bouquet in front of a crumpled old woman, taunting the patient that she was having an affair with her husband

and hadn't he sent some beautiful flowers? We all laughed, pretended it was harmless fun, but I have not forgotten the bewilderment on the woman's face. I knew this place. It had all the hallmarks of a boarding school and I couldn't wait to leave.

*

One of our patients was Gladys Spencer-Churchill, Duchess of Marlborough, born in 1881 in Paris, to American parents, who died in St Andrew's Hospital in 1977. In her biography, her mental health difficulties have been linked to her father's poor mental health, but his problems were the result of syphilis and therefore not inheritable. Gladys had a traumatic childhood. When she was ten years old, her father shot her mother's lover and she was sent to boarding school, away from the mother she loved. Gladys's mother abducted her daughter from the school, but when her father was released from prison, he was awarded custody of the children. She was taken to America, but on her father's death in 1901, returned to Paris to live with her mother. Gladys had a reputation for being beautiful as well as funny; a girl who delighted other people with her genuine interest in others.

In 1921, after being his lover for many years, Gladys married the Duke of Marlborough. About ten years before, Gladys had experimented with plastic surgery, an experiment that went badly wrong and left her with an enlarged jawline. This procedure is believed to have triggered Gladys's deterioration into poor mental health, but her traumatic childhood and unhappy marriage must have been significant contributory factors. Forced to leave Blenheim Palace by the duke, she lived alone in a house near the estate. The duke died before they could divorce and Gladys stayed on as a recluse, with only dogs for companions, until she was admitted as a patient to St Andrew's in 1962.

Gladys did have at least one visitor. Her biographer, Hugo Vickers, visited in 1975 and found her good company, still full of the charm that had once tantalised Parisian and London society. He wrote that she read newspapers and seemed aware of the world outside the hospital. Perhaps Gladys was one of the women I met, but we were never introduced.

CHAPTER 12

Work and Study

We all worked hard. Like the best of all-girl boarding schools, girl boarders at my school were expected to excel, to justify belonging to the small, exclusive club of Fairview House. Despite the evidence, I tried hard to succeed, but managed better in more creative subjects where interpretation was allowed and numbers did not feature. In subjects where there was a right or wrong answer, including modern languages, I struggled to maintain even a low average performance. The routine at school helped me study; we were expected to sit together in silence for two hours every evening to do homework, but this wasn't enough time. Those girls who were sensible enough to start their homework straight after school tried to relax after prep, meaning that the rest of us had to find somewhere quiet and private to study. Since we weren't allowed up to the dormitories, this was often a toilet or the cloakroom. The toilets were freezing, but we stayed in there as long as we could, balancing our folders on our knees and resting textbooks on the sanitary bin or the edge of the sink, until the pleading of a desperate girl forced us out. Studying in the cloakrooms was riskier, since a prowling matron would notice the light was on and switch it off, not noticing a girl tucked between the gaberdines with her French vocabulary.

Despite my plans, concentration was another matter. In isolation, without the buzz of companions, my mind drifted to any tangled social situation where I was involved. What had Craig meant? Should I have a word with Sarah about her behaviour towards Kirsty? If I walk from chemistry to French tomorrow morning, along the history corridor, would I have a chance of spotting Malcolm? Should I say 'hi' if I see him?

It was worse studying at home, where there were the distractions of television, playing with our dog or making another mug of tea. I hated closing my bedroom door, finding the silence and the low light from the high, single window oppressive. The dressing table was too narrow for my books, and I didn't have a lamp to brighten the print in my texts. I chose to revise on the stairs, hoping the family would stop and chat on their way to the bathroom.

I was lucky to have well-developed executive function skills. The executive function is how to learn, as opposed to what you learn, for example how to organise and sequence a task, knowing where to begin and when to stop, learning to prioritise, being able to make links and generalise. These are essential skills, and make all the difference to success, regardless of ability. In fact, a creative genius without adequate executive function skills would be lost, unless they were able to employ, or marry, someone else who could organise their daily life and work schedule. From my experience, the list-makers and task-finish types always succeed at work, even if they are less competent than their workmates. As a manager of other psychologists, I supervised colleagues who started tasks with enthusiasm but never finished, whose enemy was deadlines and who could be tracked down, hiding behind toppling piles of files and trays of scrappy notes. They were often excellent psychologists but found it impossible to learn executive function skills in adulthood. If you have natural executive function skills, be grateful.

Our school year was divided into two exam periods, the mocks and the actual exams, and these happened in every form, regardless of age, to prepare us for the rigours of future competitive examinations. For weeks before public exams, our lessons were entirely made up of completing old papers, which were marked by our teachers as if they were examiners. For mocks and final year exams, I made a revision timetable, covering all subject areas, and worked back from the date of the exam, dividing each day into a list of tasks. If I was less than effective during one time slot, it meant there was more to do in the next. As the exams approached, I became anxious, and the anxiety wrecked my concentration. 'There's so much to do! Scared I'll fail them all.'

We all had the habit of setting small motivating rewards. A packet of Spangles could last all day, if only two were eaten after each hour of revision. The best motivator was the ice cream man who stopped outside Fairview every summer evening. If I had achieved my targets for the day, I joined the queue outside the van, hoping he wouldn't run out of 'oysters'. These were cones shaped like an oyster, with a chocolate coating and dusting of coconut on one shell, and a scoop of ice cream and raspberry sauce inside. The ice cream was home-made, Italian gelato, slightly grainy in texture, and I have never tasted anything so good.

Maths was my problem. Although I was in the lowest set, our newly qualified teacher was one of the better maths teachers in the school, finding new ways to explain difficult problems and not giving up until we all understood. He also had a beautiful wife, something he told us often, although I didn't believe him and certainly not after their divorce. In his lessons I was usually able to follow, although I thought it was strange that he often sighed and asked me, 'Isobel, *what* don't you understand?' If I knew what I didn't understand, would I have a problem?

For exams, I practised worked examples until I had achieved a level of robotic competence, even if I didn't have a clue what I was doing, but the exam itself was another matter. If I met any slight change of format or twist in the wording, I flooded with anxiety and my ability to reason was lost in a brain-numbing fog. This is another example of an amygdala takeover, but one demanding flight rather than fight. My flight was from the past, from Miss B smacking me on the legs with a ruler and screaming into my face. The impact was in the present, right in the middle of a key exam. A pass in Higher Mathematics at C grade was a requirement for any university course, and I'm glad to say that despite my panic and sodden underwear, I achieved the required grade.

My other problem was not paying attention in lessons. It would have helped greatly with exams if I had learned more of the curriculum during lesson time, but I had mastered the knack of appearing to be listening while my mind drifted away. If I was caught out when asked a question, it didn't happen often enough to discourage my daydreaming. Without written examples on the blackboard, or in a textbook in front of me, I had difficulty processing auditory information and quickly became bored if the teachers delivered a lesson by lecture. We hadn't yet been taught to make notes as our teachers spoke.

In lessons where the teacher was not vigilant enough to scan the class or walk up and down the rows, I passed the time by reading a novel under the desk. Most teachers taught from the front and sitting with my bowed head, as if I was absorbed, I was rarely challenged. This is *not* an example of an effective executive function skill. In fact, my exam revision was not revision; it was self-teaching the entire syllabus in a matter of weeks. No wonder I panicked.

If we were forced to study in toilets because of lack of quiet areas, church was a useful revision space, so essential to my schedule that I pencilled 'church' into my timetable as a study period. The service was routine and somnolent, so there were few distractions apart from standing up to sing the hymns. In Scottish churches, pew bench ends are high, so it was possible to learn French vocab, or read from a textbook, adopting my practised head-down, eyes-lowered posture. We covered our books with brown paper, labelled Holy Bible, and made sure the cover was loose enough to swap around between texts.

No adult from Fairview accompanied us to church, but we had to avoid the eyes of other boarding house matrons or the women of the town, always keen to taunt Saggy with complaints about our behaviour.

The exam pressure on girl boarders from prestige girls' schools is well known but we hadn't heard of Cheltenham Ladies' College or Roedean. We were rivals with the girls from St Leonards in St Andrews or St George's in Edinburgh, because we met them at hockey fixtures and our teachers liked to remind us about their exceptional results. Like our sisters at these schools, we learned it wasn't enough for us to pass Scottish Highers with the best grades, we had to achieve a career *and* be a credit to our husbands, men we would only meet if we attended a top university. This was said with a glower at the boys in the class, making it clear that our boys were not a reliable source of potential husbands, at least not without pulling their socks up. We accepted that at our weddings, the new husbands would be ex-boarders from schools like Gordonstoun or Fettes, and we would execute a perfect foxtrot as our first dance. We would be doctors, teachers (promoted of course), or lawyers (family law best) but must earn less than our husbands. Our many children, all well-behaved and accomplished, would be sent to a boarding school like ours.

Despite the pressure, it was made clear we were not welcome in certain professions. Girls were not encouraged to study engineering, technology or design and these areas of the school, with teachers who wore brown lab coats and protective goggles, were a secret world of heavy wooden benches and a smell of engine oil. With the rest of the sixth form, I was bussed to Stirling University for a talk from the Foreign Office. Within five minutes I heard that women could not be diplomats, but we were cheered to learn that a diplomat's wife also had an essential role, every bit as important as being the diplomat himself. It would be such a privilege to serve the country in this way, why did the small matter of a salary matter?

I wanted to be a writer, based on two things: I wrote well, better than most children my age, and was often described as 'silly', or 'over-imaginative', qualities I guessed would suit a writer. I never confessed this ambition after an English teacher criticised one of my essays, when I tried to write a first-person story from the point of view of a man. It was red-penned because 'a woman wouldn't do that'. I didn't defend myself or explain but felt quietly pleased. In my sixth form, I wrote lots of poetry and found the courage to show them to Mr D. He gave the poems back to me with a smirk, calling them 'typical adolescent tripe', which was true.

As part of our education, we were taken by bus to the Traverse in Edinburgh or the Citizens in Glasgow, where Mr D was rumoured to be friends with the artistic director, Giles Havergal. These were both new theatres, the Traverse starting up in 1963 and the Glasgow Citizens in 1969. I wasn't impressed with the Traverse: 'It's a real drop-out hole and we were sitting having coffee when water gushed through the ceiling. The theatre is a black room with piles of foam rubber to sit on.' The social opportunities provided by these theatre trips were a higher priority for me than the play itself and a long bus trip to Edinburgh was an opportunity to sit next to a friend, usually a boy, and have a 'frank talk'.

*

The boys, whether day pupils or boarders, shoved their way to the front whenever there were demonstrations in physics, biology or chemistry. It was impossible to see the experiment, and I would lose heart, staring out of the window and relying on notes copied from the board, if there was time. In the same way, their enthusiasm to answer questions, waving their arms and clicking their fingers for attention, meant that the girls stayed quiet. This is how many boys behave when they are keen to learn, and they are not to blame. The responsible person was the teacher, who should have been aware of the problem and used classroom management strategies to make sure the girls were not pushed out.

The pressure on us to keep up, to deserve our privileged education, to make our parents proud, as well as staying desirable and sexy, did not impress the boy boarders who shared our lessons. I can't have been alone in facing negative comments about my ability or my future prospects. Other girls must also have encountered this name-calling, but we never spoke about it. It was not the fault of the boys, who were unparented, unsupervised teenagers, steeped in shared group myths about sex, girls and a false belief about what they were owed by girls and women. Being in competition with girls was not something their upbringing or the school culture had prepared them for. If we gave any hint of rejecting them, ignoring them or, heaven forbid, getting better marks in lessons, we became the target for harsh put-downs. Adolescent boys, as well as girls, need structured help with relationships, and in the absence of parents, must have mentors who are role models, who pay attention to what is happening and who gently remind and prompt the best behaviour. No adult at my school, in the 1960s, was willing to shoulder that responsibility.

My parents soon became aware they weren't getting value for money from my school, as my mother's teaching career progressed and she better understood the academic standards possible from good state schools. They tried various ways to persuade us to leave but our attachments to home had broken and we felt like strangers in our new home town of Northampton. No teenager will easily accept an enforced move of school, leaving their friends behind and facing the terror of breaking into established friendship groups. To manage such conflict, parents need determination and persistence but also to show kindness and a willingness to listen. My parents' own childhoods left them incapable of negotiating such arguments with their teenage children, since the skills they needed had never been modelled for them. The only tools in their kit were unregulated temper and criticism, terrifying for young children, a source of contempt and ridicule for adolescents and an embarrassment for adult children. In the face of their children's refusal to leave boarding school, my parents were powerless and they lost the argument, every time.

CHAPTER 13

Paid Employment

In the 1950s and 60s, school children picked rose hips for the national post-war effort to raise levels of vitamin C. The ripe hips were converted into rose hip syrup, a pink, sugary liquid, which was spooned into children in the absence of fruit. Schools acted as collectors for the Rosehip Collectors' Club and children were paid three old pence for a pound of berries. I earned a few pennies for the meagre amount I gathered but was never enthusiastic enough to try for a collectors' badge.

Children were also expected to help with the potato harvest, which is why we had two weeks off school in the middle of the winter term, known as 'tattie fortnight'. I do have memories of picking tatties but it must have been on my father's farm where I was tolerated by the professional pickers for no more than a few minutes. Whole families were collected from villages and carried on trailers to local farms, where they picked for an entire, long day. It was backbreaking work, the pace set by women wearing headscarves, their tanned skin and hard faces showing their years of itinerant work on farms. These women were unforgiving of skivers and the only children allowed to play at the edge of the field were their own.

Older children were allowed to harvest raspberries because it was piecework and we didn't hold up the experienced pickers. A farmer grew raspberry canes in the field below our house, so it was easy to earn a few pence per punnet, for as long as my stamina held out. The same fierce women, picking the raspberry crop before they moved on to the tatties, checked my work and hissed 'pick clean' into my ear as they squeezed past. This was useless advice because I couldn't reach the top ones but adults always cleaned up our rows once we'd had enough. The first few raspberries I picked were always crammed into my mouth, but after gorging myself, eating any more held no appeal. My mother was allowed to take as many as she liked from the edge of the field but we said we didn't like raspberries, so they became jam for trifles, pancakes or Victoria sponge cakes.

Once we were old enough, we were expected to find some employment during the long summer holidays. Compared to most of the population, my parents were financially comfortable, but the school fees were a struggle. Pocket money was not on offer. School friends whose families ran hotels or farms helped out at home, but I can't recall other boarders holding down a job outside the family, until after they left school. Research on adolescents and paid work is mixed. For a young person with pre-existing trauma or relationship problems, or those who struggle with organisation and concentration, paid work may not go well. On the other hand, successful work outside school can compensate for a negative school experience, particularly if the young employee develops new skills and feels the approval of older workers. Some adolescents may have to work for long hours to support their families, which affects their education and reduces opportunities to socialise with peers, but may also bring a sense of pride and independence. I recall speaking to the employer of a fifteen-year-old boy whose family were being prosecuted for his poor attendance, who praised the boy's quick retention of new skills and commented how the lad had blossomed through regular contact with adult men who 'took no nonsense' from him.

In 1969, the summer my mother spent in hospital, it was my responsibility to be housekeeper and look after my younger brother. My father gave me money at the beginning of the week, with the promise that I could keep anything left over. I took my role seriously, to the point where my sister complained that I ran the place 'like a Gestapo camp' but because I could only shop at the local Spar, it was hard to make the money stretch. If I was to save any money to take back to school, to fund my cafe lifestyle, I had to earn. I took on a paper round, rising at six every morning and borrowing my neighbour's bike. I hated the heavy papers on a Sunday and disliked the people who owned the shop because I thought they were unfriendly. To annoy them, I would begin at the end of the route and work my way backwards, hoping there would be complaints from customers who hadn't yet found their newspaper on the doormat. I was paid sixteen shillings and six pence per week.

As August dragged on, I became less enthusiastic about my role as housekeeper and childminder. My cooking skills weren't great; a typical meal for the family would be mince out of a tin, lumpy mashed tatties, followed by Angel Delight. Like most housewives, I found the repetitive tedium of housework frustrating and preferred to get into trouble with my brother. With a neighbour's child, we made hydrogen with his chemistry set, using zinc and some hydrochloric acid that wasn't included with the set but for some reason we found in my brother's room.

Term approached, and a new task was added to my list of duties – getting my brother ready for boarding school. This meant sewing name tapes onto his uniform, shopping for stationery and packing both our trunks. My mother was discharged, and although she slept most of the day, she was back in control. I resented giving up my management position and reverted to the worst of being fifteen but with added guilt: 'Why am I so grumpy, irritable and selfish about doing small tasks for Mum?' On her first day home, my parents argued, my brother cried because he'd broken one of his models, my sister made herself scarce and I managed to crack a joke, which left my mother in tears. Family life was back to normal.

The night before we returned to school, my mother said she would write to my housemistress about how helpful I had been. I wasn't happy about this, how it would be received, imagining that this information would only act as fuel for 'if only' conversations. I refused her offer.

*

Paid employment had a direct and positive benefit on my social life at school, since the money I earned funded the long hours spent in cafes during term time. My next summer job was at Marks and Spencer and required a reference from the Boss. I was in the middle of an exam in the hall when he entered through the swing doors and crept towards me over the parquet floor in his soft-soled shoes. The skin on my neck prickled as he stood just behind me, his black gown hunched across his shoulders, like a vulture over a corpse. He bent to whisper in my ear: 'I've just been tearing your character apart for Marks and Spencer.' I looked up and smiled but could only see the whites of his eyes. In almost six years, this was the first time he had spoken to me.

My induction at M&S began with lunch in the canteen. Staff food was excellent and we were given enough time to eat a full lunch every day, such as fish and chips followed by plums and cream. After lunch, we had a lesson on the cash register and a lecture about personal hygiene, including using a deodorant (with a demonstration). We were taught sales floor etiquette and how to speak to customers. If we spoke to each other, we were expected to use Miss or Mrs and not raise our voices. I was shown how to use the stockroom and reminded that I must never dawdle in there, leave my station unattended or sit down. If there was a fire, I must ask the customer to leave the store immediately, but if they refused, I should leave them to burn.

After my first full day, I realised I had replaced one set of petty rules for another. 'It's like a strict school,' I wrote. 'You're given a little dress and locker ... no talking, eating, or smoking (not that I'm worried about that). You must be neat and tidy, make-up in moderation, hair tied back, counter immaculate.' The multitasking on tights was impossible, trying to fill the gaps in my stock and keep the counter tidy, while the customers' sole ambition was to mess it up looking for their size. I quickly became competent at working out how much change to give, since the till didn't do that for us, but as well as complex mental arithmetic, I was expected to log the items I sold on a clicker device next to the till. This was our only means of stock control and I kept forgetting to do it.

M&S differed from school in that effort was noticed and rewarded. My supervisor told me I was doing a 'tremendous' job, so worthwhile in fact, they planned to allow me to stay on tights. I had imagined selling bras or dresses, so wasn't pleased. By the end of my first week, I had learned to fill up and 'click off' the numbers sold as I served customers, but all my new skills vanished on my first busy Saturday. I forgot to record sales and, as I tried to give customers their change, was swamped by my old, sweating anxiety about numbers. On the bus home, dishevelled and tearful, I wondered how I would survive another five weeks. My pay was only £8 per week, worse than the rate for my paper round.

Some weekdays were quiet, and I managed to chat with the other girls my age. One of them admitted that she couldn't understand half of what I said. There were no social worries with these girls, and I was always included, despite my Scottish accent. 'I enjoyed the company of our usual crowd at break, seven squeezed around the table!' No one questioned my unexplained absence from any local school and I started to make friends. When I passed all my Scottish Highers, I felt relief that a future on a shop floor was not mine unless I chose. I didn't say anything to the other girls because some of them had no option.

Shoplifting was a problem. Whenever I tidied my counter and made sure the piles of tights and stockings were level, if I turned back after serving a customer, there would be a deep hole where at least twenty pairs had been nicked. The early mornings were getting to me, I was often tired and made frequent mistakes with the stock lists. My old worries about being thought of as a thief crept back, and I believed our supervisor was monitoring me: 'The whole place gives me the feeling of watching me as if I've done something.' Of course, she wasn't watching me but my station, because theft from tights was worse than any other department in the store. In my final week, I prepared the hosiery counter to be taken over by my neighbour's daughter, cleaning and trying to re-stock but I had to leave the counter half empty. With relief, I wrote, 'It's no longer my problem.'

If I'd been asked, I'd have rated my experience of shop work as a failure, but Marks and Spencer thought otherwise. I was offered employment with them during any future school or university holidays, to work my way around different sections of the store until I was available to start their graduate training programme. But I could only think of a life free of tights, stock control and awkward customers and refused their generous offer, relieved that at least they didn't think I was a thief. I've often wondered about this alternative future, one where I might have bustled around an M&S store, wearing a uniform and a name badge, helping customers, or even leaving them to burn.

Instead of returning to Marks and Spencer, the summer after I left school I was thrown into the troubled environment of three different wards at St Andrew's Hospital, without any preparation or training, yet it was the temporary, student staff who had the most informal contact with patients.

On a ward for silent, slow-moving men, we washed up the dishes after tea, and I asked the nurse in charge why none of 'them' spoke. Shaking with rage, he pulled me into the corridor and in a voice quiet with anger, whispered that I was never again to speak about the patients in front of them. It was correct to reprimand me, I had made a mistake I would never repeat, but my interest in the human mind, its strengths, failing and idiosyncrasies had been sparked and I wanted to know more. Why didn't these men speak?

My final ward was purpose-built in the grounds as a modern, separate unit for short-term patients. This unit, Worcester House, was the jewel in the crown of the hospital. There was a domestic manager and rules, the most important one for those of us on the housekeeping staff was to finish our work as quickly as possible, before drinking tea in the kitchen for the rest of our shift or sunbathing around the back, where there was a hidden suntrap. My middle-aged colleagues rested outside on kitchen chairs, their tights off, pinnies rolled up and legs spread wide, revealing white, dimpled thighs for the benefit of the sun. I was only there for a week and they knew I wouldn't tell. I would try to fit in, earn my pittance and go.

It was in this hospital that I made my first friendship with a girl who was black, also working her way around the wards in her school holidays. For the few days we worked together, I laughed more than I thought possible during the entire miserable, never-ending break between school and university. There were no black pupils at my school. Some pupils were of dual heritage, but this was never acknowledged or discussed. Even at seventeen, I knew nothing about racism.

My new friend was a master of the deadpan delivery of killer lines, and her attribution of my many faults – the way I dressed, spoke, ate my sandwich, or polished the silver cutlery – to my being white made us both scream with laughter. I asked if we could meet up outside the hospital, but she refused because I was 'too white' to meet her family. It made a change to find out that my main fault was being too white. At least she didn't mock me for being a tart.

CHAPTER 14

Behaviour

Behaviour standards at school had drifted, and attempts were made to rein things in. At the start of my fifth year, AyCee called our form into her room to complain that we were poor role models for the younger girls, pointing out that our rudeness to Nelly was a good example. She announced that house rules were to be refreshed and, in fairness, we were asked for input. Our contributions aimed to tighten up everything for the junior girls but not us. We wanted them to be reminded of their place in the pecking order, resenting that they were not suffering as we had, under Saggy. The new house rules were soon forgotten.

AyCee left by the end of the year and was replaced by a woman we called Welly. Her first act was to try and impose a signing-in-and-out book, similar to one we'd had in Rosehill, where we had been expected to record where we were, who we were with and when we would be back. By this time, we were used to heading off at weekends to the local town, Glasgow or Edinburgh without permission.

Outside set times, like mealtimes, prep or bedtime, no adult knew where we were or what we were doing. From a safeguarding perspective, her decision was a timely intervention, but making sure the system worked required energy and vigilance, which no one in charge could summon and certainly not Nelly, who was often left as our sole carer. We paid lip service to recording our movements, easily finding ways to lie and cheat, and after a matter of weeks, the book lay neglected, gathering dust on the hall table.

Normally, I followed rules because I didn't want to draw attention to myself, but I was prone to episodes of risky behaviour that made no sense beyond the initial emotional euphoria of challenging the organisation. Early in fifth year, after Saggy had left but AyCee was still our housemistress, boys started knocking on the window of our common room during prep. They were out for night runs, apparently condoned by their housemaster, and one evening, as we lifted the window to chat, they threw down the challenge: 'Come out with us.'

Three of us climbed out the window, sneaking around dark streets and through the churchyard, buzzing with excitement and fear. We lost the boys, who ran ahead, and soon turned back to the boarding house, blind to the risk that we might be seen and reported by any member of staff returning home after a night out. Our friends were still up and raised the window to let us back in, breathless and pink from the frosty night. The next time, the boys arranged to meet us in the churchyard. Shoes and coats on, we climbed out of the boarding house, hurrying to our rendezvous. The boys were waiting but we didn't stay long. There was nothing to do except stand about chatting amongst gravestones and it seemed creepy and pointless. The cemetery may have been scary but the real shock hit us when we crept back to the house and crawled underneath our common room window. Lifting our heads to see inside, it was empty. They had gone to bed.

Our dormitory was in the room above AyCee's sitting room. We sneaked around the house to her window and listened. The curtains were drawn and there was no sound from inside. Was she marking schoolbooks or out prowling the corridors? We lifted gravel from the path and threw stones to hit the window above, ducking down after each throw, terrified that the sound of falling pebbles would alert her. Our friends heard the irregular tapping at the panes and leaned out to check.

We beckoned fiercely and hissed, 'Let us in!'

Moira hurried downstairs into the darkened form room and raised the window for us to climb in. I removed my spattered shoes and left them in my locker, unwilling to risk the corridor to the cloakroom, which went past AyCee's door. The lights snapped on just as my locker door clicked shut. Our assistant matron stood over me, asking me why I was up so late, at the same time as chivvying me up to bed. I apologised and rushed off, my head lowered, so that she wouldn't notice my reddened cheeks and guess that I'd just come in from the cold.

Only good fortune and chance meant we weren't caught; AyCee must have had her television on and it was a stroke of luck our friends heard the stones at the window. If they hadn't, or had ignored us, our absence would have been discovered within minutes. The assistant matron was keen to finish her shift and go home; her matron's antennae was not on full alert. Serendipity kept us safe but it could have been so different.

Like most writers, I wasn't willing to waste an opportunity to harvest my own experience for the sake of creativity. For English, I wrote an essay about a group of imaginary pupils, at an all-girls boarding school, who had a close shave, just like ours. It earned me an A+ but also an investigation into the story; was it truth or fiction? I blustered, protesting that any good writer was capable of creating a narrative they hadn't actually experienced. Since there was no evidence and I refused to admit any wrongdoing, my older sister, also known as the head girl, was asked to question me. I denied everything and the inquisition was dropped but it was made clear that no one believed me.

This pointless escapade risked all of our futures at the school, not only those who had taken part but those who colluded or had turned a blind eye. The only possible justification is the short-lived joy we felt at triumphing over the organisation. When Martha was caught climbing back into the boarding house after meeting her boyfriend, she escaped expulsion because of the impressive story she created about a family emergency and having to find a telephone box. No doubt her parents were persuaded to back her up. But going out to meet a boyfriend had purpose; our escapes to the graveyard did not. It was the last time I did anything so foolish, recognising the simple truth, perhaps later than others, that we needed to keep adults in ignorance about their laxity.

As my fifth year progressed, and our elderly matron was left in sole charge on Friday nights and weekends, skipping meals became possible, even breakfast, meaning that the senior girls were often late for church. In earlier years, missing a meal or walking in late to a church service, would have been a red flag. In March, six of us piled onto the afternoon bus to see the film *Midnight Cowboy* in Stirling, sharing a taxi back in time to catch some of the Saturday night film, which was *Anastasia*. Afterwards, we walked out of the club and went for chips, because we'd missed tea. In my diary, I worried whether our absence might have been noted because we'd been seen on the bus by the woman who worked in the post office but we weren't reported. Unlike Saggy, Nelly wasn't known in the community and rarely went out, except to walk her dog. This exploratory venture became the template for future expeditions.

For those of us who couldn't go home for days out because our parents lived at too great a distance, written adult requests for days out were still expected, but a group of us managed to hang around in Glasgow or Edinburgh almost every month in sixth form, without permission. We funded these days out by drawing on our parents' accounts. At the end of each term, they would have been presented with a bill for itemised 'expenses' rung up by their children. It didn't occur to me that it was impossible for my mother to spend a Saturday every month with a friend, shopping, having lunch or seeing a film, since every penny she earned went towards our fees.

On these illicit Saturdays, we arrived at Glasgow Queen Street or Edinburgh Waverley as early in the morning as we could manage, changing into ordinary clothes in public toilets. There was no risk to our safety. We were playing at being independent young women, not schoolgirls out for illicit thrills. Some serious shopping and a quality lunch, followed by a good film, was more important to us than alcohol or meeting strange men. We lunched like Saturday morning ladies in Muirhead's, a department store on Sauchiehall Street, or at Hendersons Salad Table in Edinburgh. If we did meet boys, they were just our boys, and not at all interesting.

A few girls from our group left school at the end of fifth year and it's possible that in this lax era they wrote letters asking permission for us to visit them in their flats. These were actually bedsits with twin beds, a sink and a couple of armchairs in front of a gas fire. The sink was cluttered with toothbrushes and soap, with a shelf holding a kettle, a loaf of bread, a box of cereal and biscuits. There was no fridge, so milk was balanced on the window ledge and the shared toilet was down the hall. We were fascinated by our friends' new lives, impressed by their newly minted adult concerns of typing speeds, bus fares and tokens for the gas meter. They made us tea in mugs, and we would sit around the hissing fire, warming up after our day wandering through the city shops. The haze of cigarette smoke grew, despite the ever-open window, blotting out the damp, sepia space our friends now inhabited. They said they were happy, glad to be away from school, but I couldn't believe this was actually true.

Smoking was the most common illicit activity at school, but alcohol use became more prevalent. In my early years as a boarder, pupils would have made desperate attempts to hide drinking and smoking, making sure these always happened far from the boarding houses. In Fairview, the 'loft' was a dusty, spidery attic above the garage, used for storing trunks. Access was easy through stairs on the outside, and in fifth form we started using it as a place to smoke and, at weekends, to invite boys. Someone would strum a guitar and we would sing along, softly of course. There wasn't the loud banter of the cafes or the simmering tension of sex, just quiet conversation between friends and the dim, smoky atmosphere of a jazz club. This was our place, one we would use again and again. We didn't bother to clear up and soon the floor became littered with fag ends, cans and food packets.

After a wet Saturday in May, we helped the boys creep down from the loft and kept watch as they strolled, unseen, onto the street outside Fairview. In our form room, the atmosphere was as chilly as the unseasonal weather, but nothing was said. The next day, we again invited the boys to the loft and had a party for someone's birthday, always aware of keeping quiet. Afterwards, once the boys were safely gone, we hurried back into the boarding house, trying to be in time for Sunday tea. We were stopped in the cloakroom by two of our year group, girls who had opted not to take part in the loft sessions. They warned us to stop bringing boys into the house. At tea, when I reached the trolley, the deputy matron, who lived in the village but helped Nelly at weekends, stared hard into my face, leaning over as she passed me my cup.

'I know what you're doing in the loft,' she whispered, her voice low but every word clear. 'Stop right now, clean the place up and nothing more will be said.'

The scone and jam stuck to the roof of my mouth, no matter how many cups of tea I drank to wash it down. Our friends were right; it was one thing to behave as we chose far from the boarding house but inviting boys into Fairview was a step too far. If we were caught, we would be expelled, which was not their problem but by drawing attention to our freedom, everyone's fun would stop. That night, we swept out the loft and never used it again.

A few days later, I woke in the middle of the night to find two boys sitting on beds in our dormitory. After the immediate shock, I felt no alarm because we knew who they were and after a brief chat, they left. With two other girls, I left the same day for our Duke of Edinburgh's Gold Award hike in the Lake District. Nelly gave us a huge breakfast and packed us off with more food than we could eat on one train journey. We arrived in Penrith by late afternoon and were stopped by the police for hitchhiking on the motorway. After questioning, they dropped us on the road to Windermere. We managed to hitch some rides that took us within walking distance, a long walk nevertheless, to the youth hostel.

The day after we returned, we walked into a storm. All the senior girl boarders were asked to see AyCee in her office at school, a worrying and unusual request. As we waited outside her office, rumours passed between us that the nighttime break-ins had continued, and the head girl of Fairview had reported the boys to the Boss. We were all interrogated, but since we hadn't been there, those of us on the Lake District trip denied all knowledge. From the testimony of other girls, it soon emerged that we had actually been in the dormitory on the night of the first visit. Now we were in even more trouble for lying. All the girls were sent back to the house to wait for the outcome of the investigation, irritating the matron and cleaners by taking up too much space as they tried to hoover and sweep around us. By the next morning, three boys had been expelled. We were warned that girls might be expelled too, but we were such practised liars, it became impossible to prove that any girl had been complicit. Someone in the boarding house must have let the intruders in, but anyone who knew, even the expelled boys, kept the secret. I never found out who organised the break-ins. Different girls from us might have whispered about the truth in huddles, but we didn't trust each other and weren't used to sharing secrets. We never spoke of it again.

I was furious with the head girl for reporting the intruders. I wrote in my diary, 'We could have sorted it out amongst ourselves and got them to stop coming up. The whole thing was so unnecessary it drives me mad.' Despite my protest, the nighttime invasions were wrong. Girl boarders had a right to a private space that was not shared or encroached upon by the boys, even if there was no physical threat or sexual intent. What emerged from this event was my lack of trust in adults to sort things out fairly. I was convinced we were in charge of our own lives and should take responsibility both for our actions and remedying those actions. By sixteen, I had no time for rules or 'management' and ever since, have had difficulty asking for help from work colleagues, line managers, or anyone else.

Although I didn't smoke and drank very little alcohol, I wanted to be included with those who did and was more than happy to take part in serious misbehaviour, if I thought I could get away with it, but I didn't like pointless rudeness or needless lack of cooperation. In September of fourth year, our voting for class captain was not taken seriously by the boys and I hated watching them vote for each other, then refuse the position. If I had been chosen as class captain, I would have accepted, but no girl was nominated. Watching the junior school concert with Harry, I was ashamed by the noise he and his friends made. I worried that young children's efforts were being ridiculed and understood the impact this might have on their confidence. Perhaps this was the beginning of empathy.

*

Sitting in the school hall, late in the summer term of my fifth year, the new prefects were read out and my name was amongst them. This was a shock, and during the summer holidays while counting stock and cleaning my hosiery station at M&S, I had plenty of time to worry about my role. Once back at school, there were new relationships to be made with other prefects, many of them day pupils I'd had little to do with in previous years. I felt caught between two worlds, keeping in with the rest of the prefects or pleasing my old friends.

I tried to walk the fine line between the two camps, and in the early autumn I carried on going behind the church with the smokers, no longer warned off by the boys, well aware of the dire consequences if I was caught. In the end I stopped, in part because I began to value the privilege of being a prefect. It was a pleasure to study in the library, even with the spectre of the Boss stalking the corridor that circled the first floor, glowering down through windows above our heads. We also had our own room for coffee, and a rota for biscuits, somewhere we could go during free periods and at break, avoiding the chilly melee of corridors where our friends stood around with their shoulders hunched and hands in pockets. But the main reason for staying behind in the cafe and avoiding the smokers was Neville, a non-smoking fifth former who had joined our group. I was more than happy to be left alone with him when the others sneaked off.

After I decided to avoid the most obvious rule-breaking, the monthly prefects' meeting with the Boss became more comfortable. Our role as enablers of discipline was enforced in these meetings, with the Boss reminding us about the need for loyalty and our responsibility in assisting the staff to stamp out smoking and drinking. Whenever he said this, the Boss would pause and stare at each of us in turn, and I always imagined he held me for longer than others in his raptor gaze.

There was little recognition that our loyalties might be torn. Most of us were relaxed about discipline and only handed out enough lines to scrape by, but those few who became authoritarian were universally disliked. Since the Stanford Prison Experiment in 1971, researchers have known that young people can become too enthusiastic about control and punishment, if provided with the right environment. In this study, student volunteers were assigned the roles of guards and prisoners and acted out their roles in a basement prison. The experiment had to be stopped because of concerns about the guards' treatment of the prisoners. None of our prefects became so extreme but there was an incident in Fairview where two prefects had to be reminded of the limits of their responsibilities, after they punished younger girls for having untidy beds. Although I gave out few lines, I discovered patience and responsibility. My supervision of prep was relaxed and gentle, and I enjoyed getting to know the younger girls, seeing respect grow in their eyes for someone who had time to listen. I never 'shopped' another pupil and always relied on my principle of dealing with any wrongdoing myself.

There was one incident I didn't handle well. It started innocently enough on a day I chose to walk out of the school grounds during lesson time with two of the other prefects. There was no plan, I simply wanted to have a short walk with friends and would have returned to the school building immediately. The chemistry teacher passed us in his car and knowing he was a staff member who rigidly enforced petty rules, I veered off from the boys towards the junior school and turned straight back into the grounds. Sure enough, a few hours later, AyCee called me into her school office for questioning. I should have said I was on my way back to Fairview, for a book, because of starting my period … anything. Instead, I concocted a ridiculous lie, saying I was collecting lines from one of the junior girls. Having involved another person in my lie, one of the youngest Fairview girls, I then had to secure my backstory. Before the housemistress interviewed her, as I knew she would, I had to persuade the poor child to lie for me and what's more, write some lines. Because I was normally kind and not too strict during prep she agreed and, to her credit, stuck to our story during her intimidating grilling. I am forever grateful to that child and learned that if you have to lie, keep it simple and don't involve others. I'm not sure what the little girl learned, but hopefully it wasn't how to become a confident and convincing liar.

CHAPTER 15

Risk

There were three incidents in my childhood where I was at considerable risk. After I started school and only my brother was at home, my mother returned to paid work. She employed a local woman to look after my brother during the day and my sister and me after school. I hated home without my mother. She was an 'old school' parent who didn't believe that children required much cuddling once the baby stage was over, but the house was a warmer, safer place with her at home. There was a familiar routine: *Listen with Mother* on the radio, baking smells, chat overheard in the kitchen between my mother and the 'lady from the cottages', my mother's rest in the afternoons.

I resented the childminder, and she developed a strong dislike of me, often shouting at me and shutting me in a freezing bedroom. In growing exasperation, she began to sit me on the cooker, switching it on for long enough so that I could feel the heat of the electric rings on my thighs.

If she didn't like the way I spoke to her, she made me lie down and fed me washing powder.

The situation came to a head when the childminder took my brother off to her own home on the bus and she wasn't there when we returned from school. In the rumpus that followed, I told my mother what had been happening to me, backed up by my sister, and the woman was sacked.

Why didn't I tell my parents as soon as it happened? Children have no sense of the power imbalance between an adult and a child. I was being disobedient, so must have deserved the punishment. There was no discussion after my initial disclosure, no police investigation, and my parents considered the matter closed. I would have liked a large policeman to turn up and take the woman off to prison. This would have helped me understand it wasn't my fault. I was at great risk from this woman, and she should have been prosecuted.

The second risky experience happened after I was taunted by a group of senior boys on the bus to our local swimming pool. They seemed to know my name and shouted down the bus, 'Isobel rides, Isobel rides, Isobel rides … a bicycle.' I was only in my first few weeks in Rosehill and didn't notice that no other girl had signed up. Once at the pool, I changed and slipped into the shallow end, since I wasn't a strong swimmer. The boys noticed me and swam over, dragging me out to the deep end. They pulled me under the water, holding me there until my lungs almost burst. Only then was I released, and my body rushed to the surface, my lungs gasping for air, emerging to the roar of water in my ears and the shouts of other swimmers. I was tossed over to another boy and again dragged down, pressed under the water with their feet. I became exhausted and knew I might drown. The next time I surfaced, I lunged towards the edge of the pool and managed to haul myself onto the side. Before they could snatch at my legs, I ran into the changing rooms.

There was a lifeguard on duty that Saturday morning, but if he noticed me at all and felt worried, it is likely he was inhibited by the loud, entitled braying of my tormentors and decided it was all a bit of fun. I almost died that day. If I had, nothing would have happened to those boys other than punishment within school. My parents would have been persuaded that my death was a sad outcome of 'horseplay' and encouraged to take matters no further. I didn't tell anyone in Rosehill, too full of shame that I hadn't guessed that swimming was unsafe for girls, and fearful I might only have myself to blame for trying to laugh at their sexual taunting. I still hate the bubbling roar of being underwater and even resist having water splashed on my face. I have never learned to swim. Although I forced myself to endure toddler water classes with my own children, any pleasure in swimming or water was over.

The last incident happened in the sixth form, and it was my brother's life that was threatened. We'd taken the overnight sleeper from Glasgow to Kings Cross many times before, since my family had moved to Northampton. Our compact cabin was like a doll's house, everything miniaturised and tucked away. We enjoyed lying awake and hearing the stations announced to empty, echoing platforms as we rocked and jolted through the night. In the half light of early morning, tea and digestive biscuits were brought to our cabin by a steward in a white jacket. We would roll up the blinds and watch the faded countryside emerge from the winter dawn.

It was late October, the start of half-term, and the taxi ranks in Glasgow had queues that were long and slow. We needed to cross to the other side of the city to catch the London sleeper, and as time crept by, I was afraid we would miss it. It was dark and late. In a crowded, busy station, we were alone. I asked Alex to stand at one taxi rank while I stood in the other line on the opposite side of the concourse. It was risky, but he was always visible to me, even if we couldn't communicate except by hand signal. Separately, we stood twice the chance of getting a taxi.

After about twenty minutes, when my line seemed to have grown no shorter, he waved to me, beckoning. There was a man at his side.

'He's got us a taxi,' my brother called out as I staggered across, dragging our heavy suitcases. I thanked the man, grateful for the kindness of a stranger. But glancing out of the rear window as our cab pulled out of the station, I saw him climb into the next taxi. I guessed he was following us.

At Glasgow Central, his cab pulled up behind ours and although I tried to walk fast, he caught up. He appeared normal, even kind and fatherly, but I didn't want any more help and could smell the alcohol on his breath. He ignored my protests and picked up our suitcases, carrying them to the ticket barrier. At last, I thought, he can't come any further. But the ticket inspector made the natural assumption that the man was our father and waved him through. Would children today have protested? I hope so. I hope they would have shouted: *'He's not with us, he's not our father!'* In the fifties and sixties, children like us were brought up to be compliant, not to question adults or make a fuss. Children like us would certainly have died of politeness, given the chance.

He can only come with us to the train door, I thought, trying to swallow my panic as he pulled our cases down the platform, my brother chattering comfortably at his side. I had relied on the steward not letting him on without a ticket, but he did. The intruder insisted on taking our cases onto the train and right into the compartment. By now I was deeply frightened and certain that he wasn't safe. I realised he was one of the 'strangers' I had been warned about for years, but even then, I thought I must be the target. Somehow, I'd only made the connection between paedophiles and girls, even though I was sixteen.

The stranger sat down on the bed next to my brother and looked at his watch.

'I bet you two are hungry,' he said cheerfully. 'There's plenty of time before the train leaves. Why don't I take your brother away with me to get some fish and chips?' He leaned across and touched my brother's cheek. Alex looked up, seeking my approval.

At that moment I understood. If I let Alex go, I would never see him again. In a split second I became an adult. Anger throbbed in a band around my head. This man must not harm my brother. I pressed the bell for the steward, desperate that he would come quickly. If we were left alone for any longer, I might not be able to stop this man from taking my brother by force.

The steward came at once, filling the doorway with his uniform, carrying authority and reassurance.

'This man is a stranger,' I pleaded. 'I want him to leave us alone.' To my relief, our unwelcome guest was escorted from the train, without an explanation or any sign of remorse. He cheerfully waved goodbye as he passed our compartment window.

I did tell my parents, but they took no action. Perhaps I downplayed the story to protect my brother, as he had no understanding of how vulnerable he had been, or perhaps I felt responsible for putting him at risk and was afraid of blame. My parents were uninterested in the detail and showed no concern that we might have been frightened. We were home for the holidays, and they needed us to be cheerful and engaged with family life.

When I think about that night, I know I almost let him go. A child is reported missing every five minutes, but most are found safe, if not well. Only about three per cent of children are abducted by strangers and our intruder was one of them. His confidence and opportunism meant he would have tried again to take a child and may well have been successful.

My brother's life hung precariously in my hands, but by chance, I made the right choice. That I might have got it wrong has been the stuff of sleepless nights.

CHAPTER 16

Health

I was a healthy child apart from a tendency to high-temperature, fluey colds, but my mental health, as a child and adolescent, was always unreliable. I had trouble sleeping at night, even as a young child, and until I was about nine years old, had a recurrent nightmare about a large, black rhino trying to force its way into my bedroom. An imaginary figure looming over my bed can still startle me from sleep and, only partially awake, I will try to swat them away. Until recently, I had recurrent nightmares about missing children, as most mothers do, and now my parents are dead, I imagine having left them somewhere or they are staying with us, and I've forgotten to give them a meal or make up their bed.

At school, I slept better than at home, finding the night-time sounds of sleeping girls comforting. At home, in my quiet bedroom, I was fearful of the silence and often lay awake, listening out for an intruder. My overriding emotion as an adolescent was one of anxiety. It was always in the background, and sometimes in the foreground, waves of stomach-clenching fear that threatened to drown me. My anxiety often settled on my health, my parents' deaths or my own, so a late period would mean that I might have cancer of the womb, or a headache meant I had a brain tumour. 'I think a lot about living and especially death, all the time.' There was a national flu epidemic in December 1969, and I was certain my parents would catch it and die. One summer I was sure I had syphilis, for no reason at all except that 'friends' from Fairview told some boys that I did. I searched our Encyclopaedia Britannica at home for details of the disease and its progression, which made me even more certain I was infected. Only my failure to develop the worst symptoms of advanced syphilis eventually convinced me I was well.

My anxiety usually settled around worries about being thought of as a 'tart', fed by the constant jibes, and an endless picking at thoughts of how popular or unpopular I was. 'I have no friends at all in this place. Why do people always like me to begin with and then get disillusioned till they hate me?' Being over-excitable and trying too hard to be funny was my baseline state but I did have low moods and often lacked hope for the future. 'I wish there was some way to prevent getting older. Why live at all? I don't belong here or at home.'

Unfortunate genetics meant that I suffered from worse acne than most adolescents, as did both of my siblings, and underlying levels of stress at school, and at home, made the condition worse, although the link between stress and acne was not recognised at the time. Stress, combined with a lack of sleep, leads to increased levels of cortisol and other hormones. The sebaceous glands become inflamed, leading to greater oil production, more clogged pores and, ultimately, huge boils, deep under the skin. The treatments prescribed by my doctor only made things worse. Antibiotics were helpful in the short-term but as soon as the prescription finished, the inflammation rose up again, even worse than before. This on/off use of antibiotics only drove the infection deeper. To the credit of the school GPs, I was referred to a specialist in the summer term of sixth year, but I went home to the family GP and then to university, and my records didn't follow me.

A consultant dermatologist advised us to use a sun lamp at home, which Peggy and I used regularly, wearing goggles to protect our eyes, which left us looking like racoons. Sunshine, or a sun lamp, has the same effect on acne-prone skin as antibiotics. There is a great improvement at first but as soon as the treatment stops, the acne returns with a vengeance. Of course, I was highly sensitive to how my skin looked but learned to use make-up from twelve years old to reduce the redness. Because it wasn't that visible and had not reached the damaging proportions of the adult acne I later developed, I was rarely mocked or teased about my spotty skin by other pupils, apart from one boy, David, who was Marie's younger brother. His own skin was prone to acne, which common sense would suggest might make him more considerate of another young person with the same problem. Unfortunately, it doesn't work like that. If a child hates a characteristic about themselves, they are more likely to taunt or bully another child who is similar, finding short-term relief through directing their pain and self-hatred at someone else.

In my late thirties, I was treated with Isotretinoin for severe adult acne, a powerful medication that directly attacks the production of sebum. The treatment is harsh, with dryness of the skin and eyes, aching joints and, rarely, unexpected episodes of severe depression. After about four months of treatment, my lips so dry that if I ran out of Vaseline, I felt close to panic, I was cured. But it was too late to prevent the scarring caused by years of painful cysts, deep within the layers of my skin. Until my cure, every day was a struggle, to face new schools, different teachers, parents and children, knowing that my scars were the first thing they would see. Sometimes, I noticed the sideways glance and for a moment thought I must be looking particularly attractive, before I remembered. The worst episode happened in a unit for deaf children, where I was observing. The children ignored me, as they usually do once they are used to a visitor in the classroom, but one little girl wanted answers about what was wrong with my skin. She asked her teachers, using signing and words, tapping at her own cheeks, again and again. The teachers were embarrassed and helpless. The child would not give up, despite being told to sit down and be quiet. Eventually, distressed at her normally kind and helpful teachers refusing to answer her question, the child had to be removed from the group. I hope that outside the classroom, an adult took the time to explain, but when I gave the teachers feedback on the child I had been observing, we all pretended it hadn't happened.

If my friends at school usually looked the other way, there were two incidents with adults that were both insensitive and cruel. Underneath my fringe was an area of skin that was hotter and oilier than the rest. My forehead was prone to spots and in absent moments, I picked at or squeezed them with my fingernails. One evening, the housemistress crept into our form room and coasted around the large table where we sat in silence, heads bowed, over our prep. I was aware of her at my elbow and must have looked up but was unprepared for what happened next. Grabbing my fringe, she roughly pulled my head back, revealing my festering brow to the room. 'And what is this?' she said, before allowing my head to flop back. I stared at my book, not daring to catch the eyes of the other girls, until she left the room. After an uncomfortable silence, they burst into laughter, and I joined in. This was our way of handling intolerable moments; we never offered sympathy or comfort but made light of everything. It was important to have a 'laugh' and then forget about it. My mother's instinct was to side with adults, and she had little interest in our lives at school, but she would have been horrified by this incident. The risk in telling her was too great; complain too much and you'll end up back at home.

The second incredible moment was in my sixth form when the new housemistress, Welly, called me into her room. I must have been suffering a bad outbreak because the reason for the summons was to interrogate me about my skin. She asked me what was wrong with my face and when I explained to her what acne was, she said, 'As long as it's not to do with not washing or your skin being dirty.' It is shocking that both women were thought to be suitable carers for teenage girls, their natural inclination always cruel rather than helpful.

This is the right moment to talk about Adverse Childhood Experiences or ACEs. There is evidence from the USA, the UK, and other developed countries that adverse childhood experiences have a long-lasting influence on a child and adult's mental health, physical health, and even lead to early death from natural causes. For example, women with just one recorded adverse experience have an increased risk of premature death. An ACE is a stressful and potentially traumatic experience that occurs during childhood and the more ACEs and their recurrence, the more significant the impact. ACEs include maltreatment such as physical, sexual and emotional abuse, neglect, domestic abuse, substance misuse (parent), poor mental health (parent), criminality (parent), separation from parents due to divorce or death and being raised in local authority care. Being sent to boarding school at a young age is not recognised as an ACE, at least not yet, but there is growing interest amongst former pupils and therapists about the long-term effect of early boarding on later mental health.

The biological causes for the long-term impact of adverse experiences in childhood is complex but in part involves the over-stimulation of the developing brain by our old friend cortisol. The child is unable to regulate arousal, suffers persistent anxiety, and continually monitors their environment for threats. The child will have problems with managing strong emotions, achieving calm or a good night's sleep. They may also 'dissociate', learning to separate feelings from experience and show only fatigue and a sense of emptiness when they try to recall the past.

It is not a foregone conclusion that a child who is subjected to an ACE will be harmed in the long term. Since ACEs are all too common in childhood, society would be swamped by problems were it not for resilience factors. The most important protections for children are known as the four Ps: loving, nurturing Parents or carers, a supportive Peer group, the ability to Problem-solve and communicate and a Passion, interest or skill that the child or adolescent is proud to have. Of course, to this list must be added freedom from the debilitating grind of poverty and the importance of a good school, with caring, nurturing staff and behaviour policies based on developing positive relationships. Information about the number of ACEs, the type of ACE experienced and the length of time over which these have occurred, combined with known protective factors, may allow professionals to predict the overall risk of harm to a child. While young children are most vulnerable to all types of harm, due to their developing brains, adolescents are known to be particularly at risk from exposure to criminality and substance abuse. The growing research interest in the long-term effects of boarding school education indicates that adolescents under sixteen are also significantly harmed by the sudden separation from home and family, by prolonged grief at their abandonment, and the resulting development of a limited, emotionally narrow, personality, to help them survive in their new environment. As well as the long-term impact of a boarding school education on future mental health, an ex-boarder's physical health in adulthood may be compromised by unsupervised and excessive access to smoking and alcohol in childhood. In this century, we would need to add exposure to drugs. Too many of my male peers from school have died early, or are suffering chronic poor health, from alcohol and smoking-related diseases.

In my own case, I have some ACEs, as do most adults. I certainly experienced abuse (but not recurrent), had repeated episodes of bullying, a few terrifying incidents where I was alone without adult support and boarding school separation from my family pre-adolescence. But I also benefitted from protective factors such as a comfortable financial background and well-developed verbal reasoning skills. I didn't have a passion but enjoyed creativity in art, immersed myself in fiction and loved social history. Although we were not naturally empathetic, the girls in Fairview House were a supportive peer group. We were accepting of each other, knew how to have fun and were united in opposition to our uncaring 'carers'.

I did not feel the support of my parents. As a young child, I believed I was less loved than my brother or sister, but it is possible they also felt less loved than me. As a watchful child, I noticed that other families, those where I stayed overnight, were more loving and less critical than mine. To my surprise, in other families parents read to their children at bedtime. I am sure I was loved, but our family was one where physical or verbal expression of emotion was rare, and love was shown through good meals, clean clothes and high expectations for our behaviour. The children of my parents' friends were often described in front of us as 'ruined' and we were proud we weren't allowed to be so chaotic. To disclose worries or distress to my parents was useless, as I was either not believed or they took no action. Adults who were meant to care for me were allowed to feed me soap powder without punishment, scream at me in lessons, or set their dogs on me in the playground, without anyone intervening. So I had to go it alone, anxious, angry, desperate to be liked (while annoying my peers) and distrustful of adults.

This is where Attachment Theory and ACEs come together. It is obvious that children with a secure attachment to their parents are far more likely to survive an adverse experience without long-term harm, because they will be listened to with warmth and supported with determination. These are the parents who will stand in front of their child's class in an old coat, an unfashionable hat, and face the bullies. Those with insecure attachments to their family will be at risk, and those children with a disorganised attachment profile are the most vulnerable of all to significant future problems with mental health. A secure attachment to parents has to be the gold standard and is of far greater significance to the well-being of a child than all other protective factors.

CHAPTER 17

Food

One Saturday in May, at the sound of the lunchtime gong, I clattered down the stairs with Moira from our attic dormitory and pushed through the door into the dining room. I was struck by the silence. There were none of the usual sounds, cutlery rapping against plates, or the babble of voices. The girls remained standing behind their chairs and only Welly, the new housemistress, was sitting down at the head of our table.

'Ah, my senior girls,' she said, as if the cavalry had arrived. 'I hope that *you*, as head and deputy head of the house, will join me for some lunch.' She waved expansively towards our places.

We walked to our seats, aware of all the eyes that tracked us. It was a hunger strike, our first experience of direct action. Unable to converse or even look at each other, we remained standing, our eyes straight ahead, the greasy, farmyard smell of hotpot drifting up from our plates. Seeing that we had chosen to side with the girls, Welly addressed the room.

'You may all leave the dining room and go without lunch. I will take this delicious plate of hotpot to my room and enjoy it there. As for you two senior girls, you are also dismissed. Please don't leave the house.'

Moira and I waited on our beds for the summons, facing each other across the linoleum. We knew that the Boss was on sick leave, so we wouldn't be sent to him, but facing the deputy head on Monday morning was even worse. He was head of maths, and his reaction the previous summer to the rebellion over the future role of prefects was now the stuff of legend.

Welly called us into her room a few hours later. We thought we would be gated for the weekend, but instead were told to see the Boss at his home, right away. We trudged the short distance to his house, rehearsing what we planned to say. It was true that we had known nothing about the hunger strike in advance, but this was our chance to fairly represent the girls' complaints about our food. We had to face up to our fear, since the Boss could be terrifying, and use the opportunity to help the Fairview girls. The door flew open before we could ring the doorbell, and if we had worried about meeting the Boss, nothing had prepared us for his wife.

Uncontrolled adult anger is an eviscerating experience and while feeling my throat constrict and a bolt of electricity stream down into my stomach and legs, I succeeded with my trick of watching her fury as if it was happening to someone else. From my distance, I saw that she loved him. This raging woman adored our stiff, distant, prowling Boss and she cared about him so much, she was terrified.

When the yelling stopped and Mrs Boss seemed calmer, she led us into a room where the actual Boss waited in an armchair. I was shocked by his appearance, writing later that he looked 'terribly ill and old'. It felt worse than the shock of his wife's anger to be told how much we had disappointed him, but we were asked to sit down while he took notes about the food in Fairview. He also wanted to know much more about the house and what we felt had gone wrong with our care. That night, I was scornful of Welly and her weakness but only told this to my diary. I thought she should have handled it on her own and only had herself to blame that we had dropped her in it.

Moira and I felt quietly proud. When the girls stopped us to ask what had happened, worrying about our future since we could easily have been expelled, we were able to reassure them. We had done our best to share their grievances and the Boss had listened. But my hopes for change were disappointed. Within a few days, blame had settled upon two girls in fifth year who were called up for interrogation. I lost any sympathy for the Boss, telling anyone who would listen that he had fabricated his illness. Not only was he a traitor but he was a shirker too.

The food in Fairview *was* awful and there wasn't enough to eat. Without any food after school, some girls' parents opened accounts for them in local shops, so that they could buy food to keep in their locker, but most of us had to manage without. My mother enjoyed cooking, so at home we were used to eating meals that tasted good. Being on the thin side and always hungry, I was resourceful in my search for opportunities to eat, offering to help at any function with food, such as the governors' tea, even if I had to serve and clear up after a group of unappreciative older men and women from the village.

Our school offered places to local children on scholarship, which entitled us to local authority lunches delivered in the ubiquitous grey, metal canisters, familiar to anyone who has visited a school canteen. On Monday to Friday, we had a 'school dinner', delivered to the boarding house. In the nineteen-sixties these were barely edible, apart from coconut tart with evaporated milk. We had 'tea' at five, which was a Scottish high tea; something light that was cooked, such as a poached egg or cheesy beans on toast, bread, fruit, and a cake. Later, there was supper, which was even more bread with jam, honey or other spreads and hot milk to make coffee or cocoa. Like everywhere in Scotland, our diet was high in sugar and sliced, white bread.

At the weekends, the food cooked in the house kitchen was usually better, but there was never enough. We filled up on sweets or tins of biscuits brought from home. One girl's family lived in the Caribbean and sent us crates of grapefruit every year. We easily ate three in one go. If we could make our pocket money stretch, we bought sweets daily from the local paper shop, scanning a tray of delights known as 'penny chews'. There was the potato, a solid, white piece of boiled sugar, dipped in powdered sugar and cinnamon, which oddly contained a tiny, plastic baby in the middle, the reward for hours of sucking. There were huge gobstoppers, multicoloured orbs of solid, hard sugar. Both of these hard sweets would last all day at a weekend, tucked inside a cheek, bathing our teeth with liquid sugar. During the week, the best buy was a quarter of midget gems, which were small enough to eat in class. If caught, the teacher would throw the whole bag in the bin, or worse, offer them around the pupils.

Whatever our age, we arrived at school with fillings, delivered by sadist dentists, grinding at our teeth without anaesthetic, using foot-operated drills. Naturally, we were terrified of dentists, a horror usually reserved for the school holidays. In the 1960s, the link hadn't been made between our poor diet and our awful dentistry. As young children, we all drank artificial orange squash, enriched with vitamin C, every day, and were given hard-boiled or chewy sweets as regular treats. Adults and children heaped sugar onto already sweetened breakfast cereals. My mother would cut lengths of rhubarb or slices of cooking apple and give them to us with a bowl of sugar to dip, suck and chew. Most of us had already had extractions, usually of decayed first teeth. At least we were anaesthetised with laughing gas for these, in the dentist's surgery, waking to hear him shouting and clapping into our faces, his expression panicked if we were too slow to open our eyes. In Berwick-upon-Tweed, our dentist's surgery was opposite my infant school. He would lurk outside the surgery at the end of the school day, to shout at any thumb-suckers he spotted, yelling across the street that he would tell our mothers if he caught us at it again.

When I lived in Canada in the late 1970s, my dentist called all of his colleagues into his surgery to observe my '1950s British teeth', a remarkable sight they would never see again. Their eyes widened as they looked inside my mouth and shook their heads, witnessing living proof of dental history, only seen before in textbooks.

My form group didn't worry about our body size or shape. Having a figure like Twiggy was the ideal, but if that wasn't our natural shape, we simply shrugged our shoulders and had another midget gem. The combination of not quite enough to eat and playing sport kept most of us thin and we didn't have any worries about whether food was healthy or unhealthy. We knew about anorexia, since we all read *Jackie* magazine, and when two girls in my form went through a phase of trying to avoid meals and restricting their food intake we kept a watchful eye and wondered whether to alert the matron. Both friends slowly returned to normal eating, without help or talking to anyone, but no adult noticed their weight loss.

*

After Saggy left, Nelly brought a different approach to meals. The kitchen was normally out of bounds and the only food available was whatever was presented at mealtimes. Once Nelly arrived, the main kitchen remained forbidden, but a smaller kitchen was stocked with Vesta curries we could prepare in the evenings, if we were hungry. I didn't approve of this being open to all, resenting junior girls crowding out the small pantry after prep.

Without a housemistress watching her, Nelly also allowed us to opt out of dancing lessons on Friday evenings.

I wasn't going to pass up the opportunity to socialise with the boys but one girl, an enthusiastic cook but a less natural dancer, often chose to miss dancing and prepare an ambitious meal for the rest of us. Despite a setback when the caramel for her egg custards turned to toffee, one Friday evening she managed to produce sausages, baked apples, mince pies, and leftover birthday cake. We stayed up most of the night telling jokes and drinking liqueurs, which appeared like magic from someone's locker, while Nelly slept soundly in her bed.

CHAPTER 18

Religion

My parents achieved an early separation between church and faith. My mother went to church because she enjoyed the rhythm of the service and singing hymns. My father held a little more religious faith, so church and Sunday school were part of my early life. By the time we were adolescents, my parents had stopped trying, partly because we lived in England and they didn't have a church to attend.

But church was compulsory at school and, in my first house, the Rosehill girls attended a small church at the lower end of the village, which may have been the original 'Wee Free' church, a smaller building without a spire, established following the separation of the Free Kirk and the United Free Kirk in 1900. Even when we merged with Fairview, we continued to worship there, along with some of the boys' boarding houses. If we had attended the same church as the other Fairview girls, our church would have lost its link with the girl boarders, and our absence would have made a big dent in the size of the congregation.

As one of the youngest girls, I had to wear the school church dress, made of an itchy, navy material with a demure, white collar. I wriggled and scratched through the tedious services under the scrutiny of Miss Kent, who frowned, giving me almost imperceptible shakes of her head, until I could at last strip off in the dormitory and inspect the irritated welts on my skin.

Once we became Fairview girls, instead of attending the church opposite the boarding house, we went to our original church without any adult supervision and were allowed to wear the standard Sunday suit worn by older girls. This was a nineteen-forties style outfit that wouldn't have looked out of place in the film *Brief Encounter*. If you had the figure for it, it looked pretty stylish. We also wore a hat, a squashed beret with the school crest on the front, which we pinned as far back on our heads as possible.

Apart from the boarders, the rest of the congregation were elderly women churchgoers, the type who sported dead animal stoles that smelt of their mildewed homes. These ladies placed peppermints in a neat queue on the hymnbook ledge in front of them and steadily worked their way through the mints during the service. Some teaching staff, their families, and matrons from other boarding houses did attend our church, which prevented most disorderly behaviour apart from eating sweets and catching up with homework.

Although I had few models of religious observation at home, like many adolescents, I responded to fleeting, faith-based emotional feelings. At the yearly Remembrance Day Service, I found the words read from 'For the Fallen' stilled for a moment my endlessly overactive brain, even though our teacher had torn apart the sentiment of the poem in an English lesson. We'd all agreed with him that the verse we heard on Remembrance Sunday was the only one worth reading. There was something about 'In the going down of the sun and in the morning, we will remember them', that poked at my repressed memory of abandonment and the loss of my family, leaving me unusually silent and sad. I also missed my grandfather, whose funeral I hadn't attended. I'd learned about his death and burial on a day out from school with my parents. Most of us in the 1960s still had links with the First World War through our grandparents and mine was one of those gassed and injured on the Somme, who survived as a changed man. The sights my grandfather witnessed left him cruel and unfeeling in his adult relationships but he enjoyed children and was able to enter our world of play and fantasy, creating imaginary stories around a character known as Jimmy O'Goblin, who seemed as vivid to him as for us. He would take us on long walks through woodland to find the goblin, who was a shoemaker, but one with a predilection for eating children. Just off the path, by a stream, there was a wooden shed and from inside there was always a knocking sound. This is where Jimmy O'Goblin lived and made his shoes. We crept up and listened, my grandfather encouraging us towards greater acts of bravery, then ran away before the goblin caught us. I think the shed was a small pumping station for water, but it was a reliable prop in our game. Was my grandfather acting out his fears, creeping up on enemy lines, as a means of coping with his wartime trauma? He was certainly unusual in his behaviour, firmly believing at times he was Winston Churchill and regaling us with stories that reinforced his grandiose belief in his own importance.

My grandmother's greatest secret was that she had spent a night in prison for not registering the birth of her first child, born before she was married. When we were very young children, staying with them overnight, my grandfather told us that our granny had been in prison and wasn't to be trusted. This was said in front of her, so that we witnessed her silent fury. I knew that something was wrong. Their dark dining room felt like an unsafe place and I wanted my parents. That was the tip of the hidden iceberg of his cruelty, his inability to manage emotions, an ordeal my grandmother endured until he died.

*

Some troubled young people find security in religious faith, God being an omnipotent, caring, forgiving attachment figure. Children and adolescents with insecure attachment profiles are more likely than securely attached children to have a sudden, intense conversion. The emotional need is to obtain security, with God serving as a loving, substitute parent figure. However, this research is based on adults looking back at their childhoods and identifying their attachment style in retrospect.

Whatever the origin of a young person's faith, religion and spirituality are protective factors in a teenager's risk-taking behaviour and positive mental health. Being part of a religious community encourages empathy and altruistic behaviour in young people but the image of God they adopt is more important than regular attendance at faith meetings. A God who is believed to be merciful and forgiving will be associated with higher levels of empathy in adolescents than for those who believe God is judgemental and punishing.

At school, we were expected to be part of the church community, but there was little exploration of faith or spirituality in lessons outside English literature. The staff may have regarded this as the responsibility of our parents, but since we were separated from our families for long periods, this was a puzzling omission.

Being part of our wee church was important to me. I had an opportunity to mix with real people from the town, even if we laughed at them behind their backs, calling the women 'wifies', with little awareness that the day we became wifies was not too far off. We were included in church activities, events not controlled or organised by the school, where there was often home baking. I attended Bible class until the end of fourth year, taught by our elderly minister, who we called Jamie, although I missed more meetings than I attended. When his wife died, he rattled around in the manse, far too old to be left on his own and we worried that no one was taking care of him. The evening he failed to turn up for Bible class, we ran around to the manse, hammering on the door, afraid of what we might find. Dishevelled from sleep, and befuddled in his reactions, Jamie eventually came to door.

He had come to no harm, but afterwards needed a leave of absence. All boarders had to attend the other church and we missed him. Even though he was boring, he was kind and tried to make us feel special and welcome. Once he returned from sick leave, we were given a choice of attending either church, but the girl boarders asked to go back to Jamie and his dwindling congregation.

I was also a member of the church choir, although I avoided most Thursday evening rehearsals. As part of the choir, I sang at annual general meetings, weddings and other special events, and was always first in line to take a package of home-made biscuits or scones back to the boarding house, neatly wrapped in a paper napkin. The ladies of the church thought no more of this gesture than finding a home for an over-generous supply of baked goods but for me, the sweet home-made food brought comfort beyond the calories, reminding me of a warm kitchen, a radio playing and the memory of mothering. I gave up church choir for one reason – the chairs reserved for us were on a raised dais right at the front of the congregation and I needed anonymity in the pews for eating sweets and catching up with revision.

I met an entirely different model of organised religion when I attended a youth leadership course at a Church of Scotland centre, just outside Edinburgh, after the Easter holiday of my sixth year. Passing the course was part of my Duke of Edinburgh's Gold Award. I was nervous about meeting two girls from my form, who had decided not to do a sixth form. They existed in the curious hinterland of 'left' but not quite gone and relations had become strained because we allowed conflicts about boys to sour a friendship that had been rocky, but consistent, over the previous six years. Because we were still in sixth form and running short of compatible boys, we thought it unfair that they encouraged our boys to date them, even though they were at college and must have their pick of great boys. They thought we were being petty and jealous, which was true.

I was glad not to share a dormitory with those two but had to sleep with twenty unknown girls. Although I was used to dormitory life, the others were not and chattered all night. There was a spiritual service of sorts in the morning and evening, with music and listening to readings from poems, books or newspapers, always with a theme and a life lesson to be discussed. This wasn't anything like the rigid format of our church services at school, with hymns sung to a sequence of numbers slid onto a wooden plaque next to the pulpit, two readings from the Bible, and a dreary sermon followed by the last hymn sung with bellowed relief. I wasn't convinced that this new place of earnest discussion, guitars and vegetarian lunches had anything to do with religion.

Our primary task for the week was to write a project on faith in the community, which meant wandering around the local town and interviewing anyone who was willing to stop and speak to us. I had my first experience of workshops and role play, joining team-building activities and trust games with awkward reluctance. I wasn't sure if I wanted to know much about my new companions, never mind trust them. All I hoped for was that the activities should stop and my own pathetic contribution go unnoticed. Presenting my findings was less of a problem, with my boarding school veneer of confidence, anticipating that my presentation would simply be heard and marked. I was unprepared for the experience of adults listening and asking difficult questions.

Something about the open, attentive attitude of the adults allowed my former friends and me to drop our defences, and for the first time we spoke a little about our shared experience of school and the boys, but it was too soon for us to have gained much perspective or insight. One thing that didn't happen was any mixing between us and the other students. On our last night there was a party, which I described as in my diary as, 'a real drag'. Freedom from the restrictions of home meant nothing to girl boarders and we retired early. Some of the girls managed to get drunk but they weren't punished. Instead, we had to endure a talk and reflection on what we had learned from the experience of drinking too much alcohol, before we wrote our log books and went home.

Fresh, bright, and free from hangovers, my former friends left for their shared flat in Glasgow, and I caught a train back to school for my final term with Neville. I'd like to say we left with our friendship restored but that would not be true. It would be at least twenty-five years before we were in touch again.

CHAPTER 19

Leaving

Some parents, like mine, wanted their children to come home. Perhaps they had returned from an overseas posting and hoped to live as a family again or had financial or marital problems. It was common for pupils to leave at the end of fifth year, because money spent on a sixth form was a luxury. In Scotland, the Highers were taken in the summer of fifth year, so it was possible to be offered an unconditional university place before Christmas. Those who were confident of their exam results left a year early, learning to type at secretarial college or earning money by working in a shop. The boys found jobs on the expanding network of motorways and within months became grown men with muscles, firm jaws and facial hair. The concept of travelling abroad for a gap year was unknown, although in magazines we read stories about girls working overseas as au pairs.

The moment the Higher results envelope landed on the doormat in August, some pupils telephoned university admissions and were offered an immediate place in October. This was not considered wise, because we were still only sixteen or seventeen. At my own university, the sixteen-year-olds, though often academically gifted, struggled socially and were often the ones found vomiting in gutters during Freshers' Week.

Those who knew they weren't coming back for sixth year, whatever their results, left as soon as the exams were over in May. This made no sense to me; their fees for the term had been paid and I thought they missed the best part of the year, the last carefree weeks of term. But for some pupils, school was intolerable, and it was better to return early to family life in preference to a few more weeks of suffering. From the perspective of attachment theory, perhaps those boarders unconsciously rejected the attachment figure of the school, before the institution rejected them. The rest of us came back for sixth form, which was only one year. It was an opportunity to grow up, sit another Higher or two, play sport, develop a new interest, be a prefect or waste time at our parents' expense.

My attachment to the school was strong, perhaps more rigidly adhered to than most other pupils, and I didn't want to leave early. It wasn't that I was always unhappy at home, as there were many times when life with my family could be peaceful and harmonious, but my feeling of alienation from them is clear from my diary: 'I realise how much I owe them but I'm not as bad, wild and stupid as they think. Mum said I was a worrying child and I'd always been the "problem" in the family.'

Family life was dominated by our mother's emotions and her personal narrative. We felt sympathy for her, 'poor

Mum' became our motto, but we were also frightened by her unpredictable, explosive temper. My father also had a temper, but it was of an endless, whiny, grumbling sort and easier to ignore. We were also scared by the part of her narrative that included dire predictions about her life expectancy, since neither of her parents lived to be old. As young children, we thought she would die soon, due to her frequent migraines, when she would lie in a darkened room for days and we would be asked to stroke her brow. She did develop very poor health during my teenage years but recovered and in the end was extremely long-lived.

My mother's emotions dominated our lives and there was no space for ours. Her story developed as the years passed and we believed that all would be well if only my father could find a good job back in Scotland, plus a larger house. After listening to my mother's sorrows for hours, I wrote: 'She was so miserable about getting old and wasting the years by putting in time here. It makes me feel so guilty to be young.' We felt ashamed of having our lives ahead of us, and not being trapped like her.

I accepted her narrative unquestioningly, as well as her argument that she was a victim of circumstances beyond her control. Knowing what I did about my parents' marriage from a very young age, and burdened with worries about her health, meant there was confusion about where the boundaries lay between parent and child, with my mother relying on me and my siblings for emotional support. In other words, we were 'enmeshed'. This is not ideal parenting practice but can be tolerable if the parent's self-interest includes the child's well-being, and care is given from parent to child, as well as the reverse. Our personal stories or emotions were not noticed or understood, a gap made worse by our long separations from home during term time. My mother showed a lifelong lack of curiosity about her children's lives, never asking questions, but at the same time worrying needlessly about scenarios she imagined.

In my late teens, my mother became jealous of my growing independence and during school holidays I had to hide letters from my friends, as my popularity clashed with her personal myth of being friendless in England. She seemed unaware that the evidence did not match her narrative. When she was in hospital for the entire summer, she had many visits from friends, neighbours and work colleagues, as well as telephone calls and letters.

Beyond my assigned problem status, as I grew older I worked hard to achieve a 'surrogate' role where I tried not only to be her friend but her saviour, seeing myself as the one person who held the simple, magical solution to her troubled life. This was a difficult balance, since in my problem role my mother was critical of me, but in her relationship with me as surrogate she was desperate for my affection and support.

In order to grow through and beyond this relationship I believed I had to stay at boarding school, and for most of my adult life I thought my parents had made the right decision about my schooling, but for all the wrong reasons. I no longer think this is true. Looking back to the circumstances of their original decision, was there really no choice? If my bullied friend at primary school, the one whose mother stood in front of the whole class, had been involved in the shoplifting incident instead of me, what would her parents have done? She would have stayed at the school, because her parents would have fought for her place. They would have had no other option.

While I was overwhelmed with relief at escaping from my bullies, I ought to have gone back to primary school. My parents should have refused to accept the head teacher's decision. Returning to school would have involved teachers, as well as my parents, being proactive about my safety, monitoring me in class and providing supervision at break and lunch in the playground. At the end of the school day, our young nanny could easily have collected me and my brother and walked us home. These would have been essential adjustments, but not difficult or expensive. Given that my parents moved to another county two terms later, before the start of my secondary education, I could have had a fresh start at a new day school, far from my bullies. As for the eleven-plus, a few months of tutoring would have ensured a pass. Everyone chose the easy way out, made possible because my parents had some spare money for fees. I lost my home, as did my siblings, but my parents lost their family, all for the sake of one bad decision.

Children learn from their parents but the opposite is also true. We all feel hopeless when we are handed a newborn baby, but we grow in confidence, our children teaching us how to become better parents. My family did not have the chance to grow together, particularly during our teenage years. My parents were too strict when we were small but they were overwhelmed by adolescents, losing any authority or power because we had become strangers, only living with them for twelve weeks of the year. My mother was very ill during my last few years at boarding school and must also have been going through the menopause, although this was never discussed. If she needed us to be at home, to ease the financial pressures on her, she should have insisted, supported by my father. At the simplest, practical level, without money worries and with children to take care of every day, my mother would have been happier and that would have benefitted us all.

*

It was a shock when a letter arrived from my parents, early in my fifth year, suggesting that I leave school at the end of the year. I blamed myself, regretting writing to them with so many complaints about Fairview, but the year had barely begun and I didn't take the threat seriously. The Christmas holidays passed without any further mention of leaving school but unknown to me, a decision had to be made by the end of the spring term or my parents would have to pay fees for the first term of sixth year, even if I had left. In March, my parents wrote just before the Easter holidays, telling me that I would definitely be leaving. My mother wanted to give up her demanding job, one where the head teacher of the school where she was deputy behaved like a bully and this pressure had contributed to her poor health. I was shocked but felt proud that by making this sacrifice, I would solve all her problems.

Once I was at home for the holiday, the atmosphere was not welcoming and I learned that a new school had been arranged for me, without any discussion. I would start sixth form at a girls' grammar school and take a full A level syllabus for two years. Even my subjects had already been decided. Throughout the holiday, I became steadily more upset, but my background had left me unprepared to trust my emotions. As my own critical parent, I tried to persuade myself that I was getting the situation out of proportion, and within the family, there was no recognition that my feelings counted: 'Mum wants me to forget all about school and fling myself into the new place.'

What parent would not hope and expect their child to be pleased at the prospect of returning home? I understood they were hurt and I felt responsible for my mother's health and the family finances. The burden became too much and I told my parents that I would leave school at the end of the year. As with all adolescents, once the decision was made, I began to settle.

At the end of April, my mother resigned from her job, and I returned for my final term. In June, during the Higher exams, my mother wrote, telling me that she had accepted a teaching position at the school I was due to attend. This was an absolute betrayal of my agreement to leave. My precarious start at a new school, the expectation that I could break into an established group of girls, was at risk of being jeopardised by having a mother on the teaching staff. I made my feelings clear; her decision was a deal-breaker. I would not leave.

Two days later, my mother telephoned to say that I was definitely returning the following year for sixth form. It was a chance for me to take my Higher French, which I had avoided, pass my driving test and, oddly, take Young Communicants classes, so that I could become a confirmed member of the Church of Scotland. The relevance of this certificate wasn't clear but it was explained to me as something I would need for the all-important, but still imaginary, wedding, which would certainly be in a church. I would have agreed to anything. I was delighted, relieved, grateful, but a small part of me wondered whether I had missed a chance for a different life. Had my mother and I been able to live together, and if I had passed A levels with good grades, the world of English universities would have been open to me.

I carried my feelings of responsibility for my mother's well-being into my final year, worrying about her 'terrible' life, but it would never have been possible for me to be the solution to her unhappiness, even if I had stayed at home for two years, because our relationship was broken. I felt sad, sorry and guilty but was selfish enough to put myself first. At sixteen, I knew what was wrong at home: 'I wish I could show more affection, but in this family, you grow up with a reserve to show anything except sarcasm.'

My mother loved me in the ways that mattered to her, the same ways she would have been shown love as a child – discipline, clean clothes and home-cooked meals. She was an early feminist, strident in her views and survived a full-time career in teaching, without the benefits of the support available to future generations. All of her salary went to pay our school fees and there were times when she sat up late at night, sewing me a dress, wrapping it, and rushing out of her school at lunchtime to the post office, so that the parcel would arrive in time for my end-of-term dance. Something had gone badly wrong in her own childhood, but she perpetuated the myth of having had a loving, kind family home, with a father who adored her. She never spoke of her mother.

My father behaved like another child in the family: competitive, teasing and irritable. Born to older parents in India, he was sent to boarding school at eight, leaving behind his ayah, and his loving but distant mother. At the outbreak of the Second World War, he was taken back to India and sent to another boarding school in the Himalayas. He tried hard to love us but had no internal model of a parent. He adored my mother, but wasn't capable of showing her enough kindness or affection, yet it was from him she should have been able to find the care she needed. They had dreadful rows, terrifying for small children, but later we became indifferent and eventually amused as they raged at each other well into their late old age. They should never have married but isn't that true of many of us?

We must accept the parents we have, in the sure knowledge that we could not have been born to anyone else. Unless they have taken active steps to learn and change, emotionally immature parents will pass on their limitations to their children, as certainly as any genetic inheritance. Unlike our genes, however, human beings are able to change their thoughts, feelings and behaviour with the support of reading, friends, counselling or psychotherapy and lead an adult life closer to the one they were meant to have.

CHAPTER 20

Bereavement, Love and Loss

It was a strange start to sixth year, discovering that two girls from our form weren't coming back; one had decided to find work for the year before university and the other planned to start her university course straight way. I unpacked my trunk in a two-bed room in the eaves, which I shared with Moira, who was head of house. As a new prefect, I was her deputy. The simple room seemed like luxury, with table lights and a window seat overlooking treetops and the graveyard opposite. Moira and I did not share a social circle beyond the prefects' room, but because of that, we had plenty to say as we lay whispering in the dark. At last, we had reached the pinnacle of our boarding school life.

The following morning, the prefects met with the Boss in the library. We were reminded of the importance of following school rules and being seen to follow the rules. We were each allocated a group of new pupils to show around the school, and later, spent time in the prefects' room, sorting out our timetables. I tried hard to be friendly but was convinced that most of them didn't like me because of my reputation as a tart.

I wandered off to find my art teacher, to talk about my sixth-form project, but he only wanted to share his worries about my friend who had left. How would she be able to prepare her art college applications and portfolio without his support? I had no answers, and disgruntled that I wasn't his main concern, decided to introduce myself to my new French teacher. This was risky, since he had a reputation for reactive flashes of temper, but he barely looked up from sorting papers on his desk and told me I'd 'little chance' of passing.

Outside school, things had to shift socially. I tried hanging out with the remnants of my previous friendship group, but they weren't happy with my new status as prefect. Marie joined our group in the cafe, and brought her younger brother, David. If he joined us, his friend Neville came too, a tall boy who wore a flop of dark blond hair over one eye. He had crossed my radar in the past, the focus of gossip because of his relationship with a sixth-former, two years his senior, who was also Fairview head girl. He was still seeing her regularly, even though she was now at university.

We were often left alone in the cafe when our friends disappeared to smoke, and he would walk me back to the boarding house afterwards. Within weeks we were a couple, but I could sense that Neville wasn't happy. He often said he was busy with sport, music practice or clubs, but Fairview girls were quick to tell me that he'd been seen hanging about with another group. When we did spend time together, he didn't want to look at me. The night he ended things, I was due to see *Rosencrantz and Guildenstern Are Dead* in Glasgow. Instead, I hid in our attic bedroom, trying to keep my humiliation hidden from our mutual friends on the coach. To my horror, I heard a creak on the floorboards outside and a sharp tap on the door. I froze, hoping that the person would give up, but it was the housemistress. She opened the door and insisted I tell her why I wasn't on the theatre trip. I cleared my constricted throat, and controlled my wavering voice, sharing only the basic facts. She offered me neither comfort nor a warning, gave a nod, and left me alone.

The following evening, as I trudged back to the boarding house on my own after a tense meeting with Neville and the rest of our group in the cafe, a car pulled up alongside me and stopped. The Boss leaned over and opened the passenger door, signalling for me to join him. I sat down but kept my body tucked tightly between the seat and the door. He asked me to explain what had happened between me and Neville, and after I finished, there was silence. He stared at nothing, as if he had forgotten I was there, and our warm breath misted the inside of the freezing window. After minutes of this awkward proximity, he turned fully towards me, both eyes disappearing into his skull, as they always did.

'You have to understand,' he said, 'that we men don't really grow up until we're about fifty.' I nodded and scrambled out of the car onto the pavement, stumbling my thanks through the open passenger window. I watched the car drive off, unsure whether the bizarre scene was a result of my overwrought imagination. It was a rare moment of kindness between me and any member of staff, never mind the Boss. Although terrifying and embarrassing, it was a significant moment, happening much too late in my time at the school. I often thought about what he'd said, and relived his awkward kindness, but I shared the story with no one. I didn't think I would be believed.

In the short time I dated Neville before our break-up, the 'whore' comments started again, from boys who still believed they had the absolute right to judge my sexual behaviour, real or imagined. The worst taunt came in a letter from Harry, by now a university student, telling me I was unpopular. Everyone was laughing at me, he said, because of the way I'd crawled after Neville.

I read Harry's revelations in the cafe after school, feeling isolated and distanced from the babble. I decided to leave, and Neville followed me onto the street, where I passed him the letter. He read in silence, and handed it back, saying, 'I can't see why Harry wants to hurt you.' Harry had to hurt me because he was unable to separate emotionally from school or easily develop new relationships at university. His attachment to the school had been broken, and he wasn't prepared for the impact of this, given his dislike of the place when he was a boarder. He was reaching back to reassure himself that he still mattered, still had importance, within the attachment culture of school. Relationship patterns developed at boarding school, like Harry's tendency to manipulate and control others, are remnants of the child's early strategy to survive. At the time, this is essential for the child, in order to adapt and fit in, but if these patterns persist into adult life, there can be a significant impact on all future relationships.

*

It was common amongst overseas boarders not to travel home during short breaks, since the cost of the flights would not be paid for by the company. Instead of flying home to the Caribbean for the half-term week in October, Neville planned to stay with Harry and David in London, so he learned of his mother's death far from home and in the company of adolescent boys. It was Harry who rang to tell me, at the same time inviting himself to my home in Northampton. By chance, the next day, I walked the streets of London with my family, the pavements piled high with foul bags of refuse due to a strike of council workers. I worried about how Neville was coping, alone and bereaved in this stinking city.

Sunday closing was still the law, nowhere in Northampton was open and I was forced to take Harry and David to my parents' house. The atmosphere was strained. My father, who easily slipped into the role of genial host following his years in India, gave them a drink and my mother made us some food but as we ate, the boys were subjected to a lecture on the dangers of smoking. I was used to my mother's lack of sensitivity when speaking to my friends, her teacher persona being the most dominant in her personality, but for once, I was grateful for her lack of tact because Harry decided not to hang around for more advice. My father drove us to the station and waited in the car park while I stood on the platform with the boys. At last, I had the chance to ask about Neville. He was with relatives in Scotland, I was told, and would return to school straight after half-term.

Back at school, word circulated that Neville wanted to carry on as before, without sympathy, and not be treated differently. For a young person who is bereaved, a return to boarding school can seem like a relief after the loss of a parent, since the parent has never been part of that community. Neville's wish to carry on as usual was respected but there was nothing more in place, such as a safe space where he could collapse and release his natural grief without peers watching, something not easily available for a boarder living in a confined space.

Adolescents experience the full range of grief, like everyone else, but there are unique stresses for this group following a parent's death: possible regrets about rows before the parent died, worries about how to protect the living parent and guilt about following interests or seeing friends. In school, there can be difficulties with learning, particularly concentration, and their progress may falter. The key thing is to encourage the young person to talk about what they need and be flexible in adjusting their school day.

The unique stresses of adolescent bereavement are compounded for boarders, since the deceased parent has never been present in the young person's life at school. I remember the shock of bumping into my mother on the street outside a cafe where I had just left Neville. She seemed like an apparition, as if I had bumped into my dead grandfather. I was aware she was spending the weekend with my father in a local hotel but hadn't worked out that weekends included Friday night.

The grieving process for a boarder can be especially complex. In term time, the child might survive in a state of denial, to be faced every holiday with the fresh shock of unprocessed grief. The young person will need trained adult support to maintain contact with the widowed parent, who might live overseas, and help to hold the deceased parent in mind, in a place where the mother or father existed as no more than a shadow. In the Department for Education's 2022 minimum standards for boarding schools, I could find nothing about supporting a child following a bereavement, yet such bereavements will not be infrequent and are likely to require specialist support.

One member of staff did seem to be monitoring Neville. After the break-up, we continued to be close friends, if not lovers, and on two occasions when we stood on the bridge over the rushing stream that bisected the village, our heads close together, Mr D slowed his car and stared. Was he thinking I shouldn't be spending so much time with Neville? When I noticed us being observed, that was the conclusion I reached. I wanted to help, but my own experience of dealing with bereavement, with Janet, Miss Kent and my grandfather, was to turn away and pretend it hadn't happened. Neville was only a few weeks past the death of his mother and a quiet chat with Mr D would have helped me support him in the right way. This didn't happen and I muddled on alone. I tried to listen, but was so enmeshed with my own mother, I almost always ended up talking about her. There were times when his mood became dark, and in early December I wrote in my diary that he seemed 'close to despair'. I tried to understand, but typically assumed his moods were my fault, floundering to find the best way to help.

*

Christmas came and my own holiday from school felt happier than the previous year, perhaps because my mother was settled in her new job and her health was stable. The house felt calm, warm and peaceful, the winter weather was perfect, with frozen ponds and frost on the trees. I took long walks with my brother and our dog, or sat around the open fire talking to my sister, but I couldn't explain to anyone what had happened to Neville.

The pre-Christmas truce with my mother didn't last. I fell out with her about her plan to write to the school with a list of complaints, arguing that such a letter would hardly make life easier for me, since I was still attending. My parents also had some ferocious rows, where both said some pretty awful things. I wrote: 'Mum stayed in bed all day with a migraine. We forgot Dad's birthday.'

After the Christmas holidays, the Boss asked to see me. I was terrified he was going to talk to me about Neville, that he intended to warn me to stay away, but he only wanted to ask about Fairview and how things were going with our new housemistress. This was a surprise in itself, but it would have been better if we had talked about Neville. I had already discovered the Boss's hidden kindness, and he would have been the right person to have this conversation with me, if only I could have trusted him. I needed adult support but couldn't risk Neville's future at the school. Had I told the truth about his dark moments, the troubled thoughts I had read in his writing, he might have been sent home and our friends would have considered this a betrayal.

In January, Neville had his seventeenth birthday, but I was still sixteen, not turning seventeen until March. Although I was a year ahead of Neville, he was older than me because of my unfortunate promotion at primary school. He had spent his first family Christmas without his mother, and as the spring term began, things didn't go well. When we met in the cafe, he was either silent or unpleasant and the atmosphere between us became strained. If I thought I was coping with Neville's volatile moods, I wasn't prepared for what happened next, a frightening escalation of his anger.

Why didn't I walk away? This was my second destructive relationship and while Neville was not controlling or manipulative, when he was angry with me he could be cruel. In my diary, I recorded his words and while I protest, my lack of a response in my own defence, indicates my limited emotional range. The school had done its work.

From a fifty-year perspective and with the understanding of a child psychologist, I can see that Neville trusted me enough to behave in a truly awful way, knowing I would still care. He was furious with me for my failure to look after him, to nurture him, to be more generous with touch than I was reputed to have been with other boys, but I did not have an adult perspective. Neville's behaviour simply confirmed my already low self-belief. In other words, I thought I deserved to be treated this way. I had been taunted for years about being a whore and a tart, so why should Neville treat me any better?

*

Managing the remaining parent is difficult for any bereaved adolescent and Neville was honest about how hard he found it at home without his mother. Natural, uninterrupted development allows a young person to break away from parents, confident of their ongoing support at home. But a bereaved parent may reverse the adult/child roles for a while, seeking care and comfort, which in turn can leave the adolescent feeling responsible, trapped and angry. This is what Neville must have faced during every break from school. Even if emotions weren't my strength, I had the boarders' knack of trying to find practical solutions and I worked out that it was time to take a risk and make our relationship physical. I couldn't help with his bereavement, but finally, I thought I knew what was needed.

I arrived home for the Easter holidays, my final holiday from boarding school, exhausted after a long train journey with changes and diversions, in a panic about my sixth-year dissertations. For the last few days of term, I'd been in a fever, trying to submit them on time and I knew they weren't good. Regardless of the dismal content, I'd paid for typing and it was a mess. My parents had allowed me to have a sixth form, I'd made Neville my priority and now I was facing the consequences.

Lying in bed in the early mornings, listening to my family slowly waken, I fretted that Neville didn't telephone me: 'To him it's probably a short time but to me it seems like years. I feel so empty and lonely, as if suspended in some unreal world.' I had no insight that Neville, immersed in his family's grief, might have felt embarrassed to ring a girlfriend in front of his father. In those days, telephones were always in the hall, and conversation was never private.

For the first week of the holidays my mother was at work, and I enjoyed lazing around the house with my brother and avoiding revision for my Higher French. My mother's health deteriorated, and once her own school holidays began, we soon quarrelled about my lack of schoolwork. It was hard enough managing my conflicting feelings of resentment and guilt, but when it was hinted that I should think about leaving school after my exams, my response was a hurtful and emphatic 'no'. I would not miss my final weeks with Neville.

My mother was so ill, time spent in bed was essential if she was to be well enough to start the new term. I did try to revise French, but couldn't concentrate, distracted by games of chess with Alex, reading novels and making cups of tea. Having no local friends, we often took the bus into the town centre, to wander around, have coffee and window shop. It was unremarkable but no less disgusting that on one of these bus journeys I had to endure the man sitting behind leaning forward to stroke my hair. We didn't move away; such a mauling was only to be expected. If I didn't want to be touched, I shouldn't have long, shiny hair that smelt of herbs.

At the start of term, shredded with excitement at seeing Neville, I dropped any resentment about my letter-free holiday. We were able to meet after lunch since lessons were only planned for half the day, and although I was crippled with period pains, I thought the afternoon started well. Without warning, Neville fell silent, the colour drained from his skin, and he turned grey. He wouldn't speak, except to say he had feelings that 'something was going to happen'. I sat down next to him, gripping tufts of grass at my side. Slowly, Neville's pallor reduced and his gaze focused, but he couldn't explain what had happened. I blamed myself and was sure that he no longer wanted to be with me, but that wasn't the reason. The school holidays had been a struggle; his mental health wasn't improving. He needed help but neither of us knew how to ask for it.

The pressures on us both went beyond bereavement. The boys Neville lived with provided a constant stream of negativity about me, and with his already low mood, this troubled him. David, Neville's closest friend, couldn't hide his dislike, walking out of the cafe whenever I entered. One afternoon in history class, David passed by our window with a group of his friends. He glanced up, spotted me, and said 'puke' loudly enough for me to hear. Of course, one of my male classmates told me the comment had most definitely been intended for me.

Neville was doing his Highers, essential for applying for a university place the following year, and I desperately needed a decent grade in my Higher French to study English at St Andrews. I decided that we should spend more time apart for exam revision and whether it was the break, being away from his family, or simply settling back into the term, Neville's mood improved.

As the exam period ended, evenings lengthened and many of our friends left school. During the day, I spent my time with the other prefects and my evenings with Neville, although we were rarely alone. Cricket was his passion and it had to become mine. I spent long summer evenings watching endless games, with the school team in field, the sun setting behind their long shadows.

Neville returned to himself, the young person I had first met, confident with friendships, neither attention-seeking nor dismissive and never controlling or bullying towards others. In other words, he was secure in his attachments. This was not a boy who would go back to the boarding house and recount in technicolour every item of clothing removed, or body part touched. I learned to trust him, forgave his behaviour and dropped my habit of anxiety-based prodding at our relationship. We became close: 'All the barriers are down, we can't hide anything from each other and have no more need for defences. He hasn't had a depression for ages and we both feel at ease in each other's company.' By the end of term, we could not imagine a world without each other and started to make plans for our future together.

*

Shortly before school ended, my mother came to Edinburgh to watch me receive my Duke of Edinburgh's Gold Award. I wasn't wearing my uniform summer dress because the only clean one I owned had been soaked with tomato juice the day before, when I helped prepare sandwiches for a governors' event. The boarding house staff didn't think to wash another one for me, even for such an important day. If I sound helpless for a seventeen-year-old, this was true. We were not allowed access to a washing machine or an iron, and had to rely on the whim of an adult to remember an important day and ensure I had the clothes I needed. That is how paid adult care works.

My mother was furious about my heavy clothes, a uniform at the end of its life, my skirt held together with a safety pin, covered by a jumper full of holes. I pretended not to mind as I sweated in the hot sunshine, waiting in a row alongside at least a hundred other students in the grounds of the Palace of Holyrood House, before stepping up to the podium and accepting my award. Over dinner, I tried to explain to her about Neville, but she was angry about her disappointing visit and said she wouldn't be pleased if I was miserable once I came home. Any possibility of sharing my worries about separating from Neville was blocked.

On my last night at boarding school, I tried to join in with the traditional revels but, in my preoccupation with Neville, had forgotten to keep up with friendships and found only groups of leavers I hardly knew roaming the streets, drinking beer from bottles and singing, as if they were celebrating. The ex-head boy offered to buy me a drink in a nearby pub and after a quiet, solemn pint, I asked to be dropped back at Fairview and went to bed. At dawn, high above the street in my attic room, I watched my year group dance a Scottish reel in the street, a pointless tradition meant to wake the girl boarders, a relic from the days when female leavers were not allowed to join in the leavers' night celebrations. Moira did not return until breakfast, cheerfully telling me about a party for prefects that had rocked all night, hosted by one of the younger staff members.

The new prefects were already in charge. I had deliberately failed to order my father a ticket for the prize-giving, trying to keep home and school separate for a few more hours, and hid from his voice, rising above the noise of the crowd as he argued with staff about his right to a seat. He was eventually found a place and after the ceremony, I tracked down Neville amongst the new prefects and introduced them, watching Neville roll his eyes as my father called him Stewart. My father left to find Alex and I joined the line in the library to shake hands with staff. A few clasped my hand firmly between both of theirs, pressing down hard, others barely touched me, but I felt dazed and incoherent, and the moment of farewell passed too quickly. Snatching a few more minutes alone, I tried to find any remaining friends to say goodbye but the prefects' room stood empty, stripped of notices, swept and unnaturally clean. In the corridors, amongst a crush of pupils and parents, there was no one I recognised. My father waited on the school steps, keen to start the long drive home. Alex was already in the car and Neville had gone. There was no need to go back to Fairview, my trunk had been despatched days before. Hollow, empty and numb, I began the long drive home.

CHAPTER 21

The End

I didn't see Neville again for at least two months and the worst of my mother's warnings about my mood were fulfilled. I was often tired, my movements sluggish, and I felt separate from my own life. The feeling of being at a distance from normal time meant that I only wrote in my diary sporadically, so there is little record of how I passed my days. Working in the psychiatric hospital for the summer provided little relief from my most gut-wrenching, heartbreaking problem – the cool, distant tone of Neville's few letters. In one, he told me he'd been spending time with boys from his boarding house who had been goading him that I would drop him at university. I knew I shouldn't write begging, crawling letters back, but I wasn't successful.

Neville wrote before I left for a family holiday in Scotland, letting me know that he wouldn't be able to see me at the former pupils' weekend in early October, just before I started university. I had pinned all my hopes on that date but he had already arranged to go home for the weekend. This moment was the beginning of our end, a trail that began with sexual bullying and coercive control from Fisherman and his cronies, the entitled taunts about my sexual behaviour from boy boarders, and Neville's treatment of me during his worst months. Confined at home, I felt powerless and full of self-hatred: 'Looking in the mirror, I'm so ugly I'm not surprised that Neville is having doubts.' I could be clingy and demanding, but within me there was always a deep, hidden anger. At this moment, even though I hated myself, I felt a furious resentment about the way I had been treated. Our future together was no longer certain.

In the end, we did meet at the former pupils' weekend, but with little time alone it was hard to find each other. Surrounded by friends, the formal activities of the weekend and the demands of school routine, which still applied to Neville, we snatched at, rather than caught, the magic of the last weeks of our relationship. Even as we held hands walking back to Neville's boarding house, so that he would be in time for tea, we were accompanied by David, vomiting into the gutter. Marie was also there for the weekend, already pregnant with her first child by the boy she had met in sixth form and was to love for the rest of a long and successful marriage. That night, we lay awake in our shared hotel room talking about our hopes for the life ahead, and I secretly wished I had a bond that would tie me to Neville forever, if only as shared parents of an unplanned child.

Within days, I was alone in a sterile hall of residence room, with my trunk beside me, without Neville, my family or my school. But Moira was there, and with a day pupil from our school called Catriona, we formed a trio and bravely went together to Freshers' Week activities and society parties, pretending to be having a wonderful time. In fact, my course was going badly. I had no Latin, so had to take extra Latin classes. Through rote learning and diligent memorisation of my vocab in church, I had achieved a B in Higher French, but no one at university would listen when I said I couldn't speak or write French, and I was forced to take first year modern languages.

My lazy sixth form had left me unskilled. In lectures, the modern history lecturer spoke with such speed, I couldn't keep up with writing notes and his rattled spiel was about people and events I'd never heard of. In English, we studied Late Old English and Early Middle English, not the twentieth century plays and poets I was used to. Languages had never been my strength and I was cornered onto a degree course in foreign and ancient languages.

We mixed with young men and women from English schools, most of them older than us, having done Oxbridge entrance and failed, followed by that strange thing called a gap year, which they liked to talk about at length. To our surprise, we discovered we were popular. Our education had given us a veneer of independence that girls from single-sex schools lacked, and we showed a relaxed confidence with boys. Soon we were part of a friendship group that drew us into the heart of university life. I was given the nickname Rags, other students seemed to find me interesting, and I felt the tart/puke girl drift away. School had left me with a weak sense of self and I grasped at any certainties, desperate to adapt to the people around me and be included.

To be able, at last, to turn my back on sexual bullying and the shame that accompanied it led to the end of my relationship with Neville. He belonged in the culture of school, was influenced by the views of other boys and his best friend had latterly become my worst critic. If I stayed with Neville, I reasoned, I would never escape the role I had been assigned. I didn't end my relationship with Neville, I ended my relationship with school.

It didn't have to happen. It was too important to get wrong. We may have grown together or grown apart, but young love has as much chance of surviving as any other relationship and should be given a chance. But my experience of sexual bullying at school affected my decision in ways that are only possible to see with hindsight. I could not tolerate the risk of further manipulation, bullying or control from his friends, or survive the self doubts their views engendered. I hated becoming the woman his friends had warned him about, someone who would dump him as soon as I met other, more desirable men but I was a prisoner of the crippling effects of past experience and a desperate need to belong to my new friends, to connect with their attitudes and beliefs and most importantly, hide from emptiness.

My boarding education left me broken in ways that only became clear as the decades passed: long-term difficulties with relationships, poorly developed empathy, a pseudo independence and competence, a desire to avoid conflict at all costs and a problem knowing myself and asking for what

I needed. The two closest relationships I had with boys at school left me with a narcissistic belief in my competence to manage young men with problems, instead of running for the hills to find kind, uncomplicated relationships without coercion or anger. This was not the fault of the young men, who were both deeply troubled for different reasons, but the outcome of unsupervised relationships without adult support, monitoring or intervention. It is possible that such intense peer-on-peer relationships, taking place outside any family structure, may be more powerful and have longer-lasting impact than typical teenage relationships between adolescents who live at home. I have no evidence of this, but my psychological backbone warns me that this may well be true.

There were few of the promised advantages of boarding school either. I passed my exams well enough, but I expect I would have achieved average grades anywhere. I left school without an interest in sport or any enthusiasm for a hobby or musical instrument. There were no social advantages, not even knowing how to dance a quickstep, nor did my old school network provide a leg-up into my chosen career, not that I would have wanted that. The only piece of advice that stuck was the Boss's insight about men.

CHAPTER 22

So What?

Does any of this matter now? Boarding schools have changed, haven't they? If we watch videos of current young boarders, they seem happy, bouncy children, running in from the playing field to chatter over tea, before piling into dormitories, perhaps to have a pillow fight, before being tucked up in bed with their teddies. This publicity misses the point. Children are meant to be raised by a parent or parents. To survive their catastrophic abandonment, young children adapt and will create a new boarding school persona, one which will look to an observer as if the child has 'settled'. Schools argue that pastoral support is 'wonderful' these days, but the settled children will never come to the attention of school therapists or counsellors. Problems occur when the child goes home; the parents have not travelled on the child's path and will expect to welcome home the child they left behind. Acutely aware of this, the child struggles to become the person they once were and ends up living between a home self and a school self.

I recently watched a documentary where a parent spoke about how boarding school allowed them both, the child and parent, to experience the best of each other; in other words, they had both formed an inauthentic personality, one that survived without arguments or quarrelling. Part of growing up is to fall out with your parents, particularly in adolescence, and learn how to resolve conflict and make repair. The absence of the rupture and repair cycle, in families who only see their children at weekends or in school holidays, who strive for everything to be 'nice' during these visits, may be one of the most damaging aspects of a boarding school education. Learning how to repair when things go wrong is essential for developing confident relationships and good mental health into adult life. A child does not need parents who are perfect but parents who make mistakes, perhaps even shouting and being critical, but who know how to quickly apologise and model how putting things right. Without regular experience of rupture and repair from adults, the ex-boarder is left without the skills and confidence to manage relationships in the future, particularly conflict.

Not everyone who attends boarding school is harmed by the experience but the evidence for categorising early boarding as an adverse childhood experience (ACE) is mounting. Children who survive boarding school relatively unscathed are likely to be those who had a positive relational start at home and started boarding at a later age. Young children at boarding school, typically those of primary school age, are potentially at risk of later mental health and relationship difficulties and all staff who care for them should be trained in trauma-informed, relationship-based approaches. Those children lucky enough to have enjoyed good enough early parenting will have developed a brain structure and firm neural pathways that allow them to easily make new secure attachments and be less at risk of long-term harm, but no young boarder will escape feelings of abandonment, grief and broken attachments. Nurturing approaches from trained staff will help all young boarders to make the best adjustment possible.

The negative effects of a childhood spent at boarding school on future emotional and social relationships can be deep, particularly for adults who were sexually or physically abused or bullied at school. I would add to this hidden peer-on-peer abuse: boy to boy, girl to girl and boy to girl, including the sexual bullying of girls by immature boys. Adult problems on leaving school may feel like quirks of personality, of unknown origin, until long-term depression and anxiety drives the ex-boarder to seek help. An insightful counsellor or therapist will help to make the link back to abandonment and broken attachments. All therapists and counsellors should ask adult clients if they attended boarding school and take on additional training or reading to help support their client, if this is the case. No one wants to accept that they were harmed by their parents' choice of school, particularly if the myth of a privileged education has been swallowed wholesale, and because of this denial, ex-boarders can be a difficult group to work with.

My habit of dissociation started at boarding school but is not without benefit for a writer, which I have eventually become, one who chooses to opt out of the present into a different world. I am easily overwhelmed and, until therapy, did not understand why I became exhausted and wanted to leave social events long before everyone else. I hate difficult emotions and like to keep all relationships smooth and safe, meaning that I avoid uncomfortable conversations and fail to confront insensitive or hurtful behaviour from others. If I do try to challenge, my attempts almost always make things worse. I find it hard to be sure of what I'm feeling and my emotions flit around, so I can't be confident about which feelings really matter. With these deficits, I haven't been great at helping my children grow into socially competent and emotionally agile adults, but I've certainly been a whole lot better at this than my own parents were. The weirdest behaviour I can lay at the door of boarding school is my failure to genuinely welcome home close family if they've been away for a while. Instead of being excited and showing delight, I become withdrawn and business-like for the first few days. This is a lifelong response to my early abandonment. As a grandparent, I have become aware of feelings of 'overwhelm' if I am with grandchildren all day. I adore my grandchildren but these feelings arise from the conditions I experienced at school, where there was no escape from social contact until we were all asleep.

I would not recommend boarding for any child but do accept that some parents work such ridiculous hours that from Year 9 onwards it may be best for a young person to board at school, if the alternative is to come home to an empty house every night. For this group, weekly boarding may work, as long as the parents commit to a full and active family life at weekends. It is never possible for paid adults to notice and respond to children in the way that a good enough parent would. In the best of schools, and even in a weekly boarding context, small but significant oversights and neglect will always occur within group care. It helps if the adolescent has full access to their mobile phone, allowing a quick conversation with a parent. Children should also be encouraged to tell an offending adult how they feel, confident that the adult will listen and model repair.

In all boarding schools, whether single-sex or co-ed, adults must monitor adolescent relationships, whether friendships or romantic pairings, and be particularly vigilant about coercive control. Coercive control has become worse for adolescents since the advent of easy access to porn and dubious internet influencers. The mission statement of the school should include a clause: 'We look after children on behalf of their parents and are responsible not only for their education, but for their emotional well-being, mental and physical health and their future strength and confidence in relationships. We aim to do this better than the very best of parents.'

In terms of bullying, intervention must go well beyond an anti-bullying policy. The school should work hard to create a culture of telling, where pupils feel empowered to report anything that makes them feel uncomfortable or unsafe. All school staff, including cleaners, cooks, coaches and teachers should have training on providing a nurturing school environment, based within an understanding of child development and relationship-based approaches to learning and discipline. If this training seems difficult to access, approach a local authority or independent educational psychology service. It is essential to include every member of staff so that no child ever again hears the cruel words spoken to me by a member of the kitchen staff. The adult a child might turn to for help cannot be assumed from their designated role. If this is a groundsman/woman, a teacher, or a technician, these adults need the right training and to know where to go themselves for personal support. It could never have been predicted that our terrifying head teacher was the most caring member of staff I encountered. If he had held the door open a little wider and I had learned to trust him, how different my school experience might have been.

In a boarding context, as in all schools, bullying will often be hidden by the child because of shame or a fear of making things worse. Adults must observe the children or young people in their care for signs of any child being left out, appearing tearful, lonely or changed. Ask questions in a thoughtful, enquiring way; for example, 'I'm wondering if …', or 'I noticed that …' and leave the child plenty of space to reply. Even if the child denies being bullied, trust your instinct, and bring the bystanders onside through empathy-based approaches. Training on anti-bullying and restorative justice approaches is essential and will be available from an educational psychology service.

There is a view that boarding school is equivalent to foster care. This is not the case. Children in foster care will have experienced years of chaotic neglect, domestic violence, parents who misuse drugs and alcohol and sexual or physical abuse. They will not return to their homes in school holidays, as boarders do, and any return to their parents' care will be the outcome of long-term planning. A foster child may have frequent moves between care settings, including changes of school. At eighteen, they will be expected to fend for themselves. Making the comparison between the lives of children at boarding school and children in care, minimises the degree of trauma that a care experienced child must overcome and is unhelpful for care leavers.

It has been suggested in the literature that boarding school might be a helpful alternative for a child who lives in difficult circumstances at home. Should the child meet the threshold for the intervention of statutory services, Social Care is the appropriate agency. If the child's family problems are not severe enough for Social Care involvement, boarding school will only provide a temporary reprieve, as the child has to return to their parents in the holidays. In my case, critical, emotionally unregulated parents were replaced with critical, unregulated adults at boarding school, so there was no reprieve, only confirmation that adults were self-involved and did not have a child's best interests at heart. I have also read a suggestion that parents considered unsuitable to provide the background support a child at boarding school needs, should be screened out and their child refused a place. Not only would such an interview or questionnaire have little validity or reliability, I cannot imagine any school being willing to take on the responsibility of informing prospective parents that their parenting skills were found to be so weak, their child could not be accepted. Fifty-two weeks a year boarding placements exist, but these are typically highly specialist environments for vulnerable children with complex needs and usually require a statutory Education and Health Care plan before the child can attend.

If any parent reading this is considering boarding education, try to ignore the school's publicity and the opinions of your friends and family, particularly if you live in an environment where boarding is the norm or you have a family history of boarding. If you boarded yourself, or your parents did, ask the question: 'Did it really do me/them no harm?' With the child's other parent, question what it is about your own parenting you believe isn't adequate to prepare your son or daughter for the years ahead and why you think strangers can do this better. Are qualities of resilience and independence really your top priority for your child's development?

A young child may beg to be a boarder, but it is important to remember that boarding school stories are fiction, usually written by authors who were not boarders themselves. You are the adult; a child can be asked for their opinion but a decision about their future schooling belongs to the parents alone. Read widely and include recent memoirs written by ex-boarders and the growing body of research about the harms done to children through boarding school education, particularly young children. If you still decide to send your child away, wait until Year 9.

I attended a good school, which is now an excellent school. It would still be an exceptional school without boarding pupils, or at least with boarders only in the sixth form. It is unlikely this will happen in my lifetime, but if we can at least end the abuse of early boarding, more children will have the chance to grow into the adults they were meant to be.

FURTHER READING

If you want to read more, here are some books, articles, reports and podcasts I would recommend:

1. Beale, Charlotte, *Boarding Schools are Bad for Children. Why do they Still Exist?* MadintheUK.com. 2022. Available at: https://www.madintheuk.com/2022/12/boarding-school-bad-children-syndrome/

2. Cavenagh, Penny, McPherson, Susan and Ogden, Jane, *The Psychological Impact of Boarding School – The Trunk in the Hall.* Oxford: Routledge, August 2023.

3. Cross, Piers, Transformational Coach and Therapist. *The Evolving Man Podcast*. Available at: https://www.piers-cross.com/an-evolving-man-podcast

4. Department for Education. *Boarding schools: national minimum standards*. 2022

5. Duffell, Nick, *The Making of Them: The British Attitude to Children and the Boarding School System.* London: Lone Arrow Press, 2000.

6. Graham, Ysenda Maxtone, *Terms & Conditions, Life in Girls' Boarding Schools 1939–1979*. London: Abacus, 2017.

7. Howe, David, *Attachment Across the Lifecourse: A Brief Introduction*. London: Red Globe Press, 2011.

8. James, Gregory, 'The Psychological Impact of Sending Children Away to Boarding School in Britain – is there cause for concern?' in *The British Journal of Psychotherapy*, 39 (3), (2023), pp. 592–610.

9. National Education Union and UK Feminista, *It's Just Everywhere – a study on sexism in schools and how we tackle it*. 2017. Available at: https://ukfeminista.org.uk/wp-content/uploads/2017/12/Report-Its-just-everywhere.pdf

10. Partridge, Simon, 'Boarding School Syndrome: reconsidered in social context and through the lens of attachment theory' in *New Directions in Psychotherapy and Relational Analysis*, 15, (2021), pp. 269–278.

11. Petter, Olivia, journalist and author of *Millenial Love*. Fourth Estate, July 2021.

12. Renton, Alex, *Stiff Upper Lip*. London: Weidenfeld and Nicolson, 2017.

13. Simpson, Nikki, *Finding Our Way Home – Women's Accounts of Being Sent to Boarding School*. Oxford: Routledge, 2019.

14. White, Amelia: *What's it Like for Girls?* BACP Children, Young People and Families. 2022. Available at: https://www.bacp.co.uk/bacp-journals/bacp-children-young-people-and-families-journal/december-2022/articles/whats-it-like-for-girls/

15. Women and Equalities Committee, *Attitudes Towards Women and Girls in Educational Settings.* UK Parliament. 2023. Available at: https://publications.parliament.uk/pa/cm5803/cmselect/cmwomeq/331/report.html

16. Zeedyk, Suzanne and Partridge, Simon, *The sciences of ACEs and attachment insights into their shared history in Scotland and beyond.* 2023. Available at: https://communityjustice.scot/wp-content/uploads/2023/10/ACEs-Attachment-Zeedyk-Partridge-2023.pdf

APPENDIX I

Hard to believe, but there was a world outside.

Concorde's inaugural flight: 2 March 1969 – 'I forgot to mention that the Concorde went up on Sunday.'

General Eisenhower died: 28 March 1969 – 'General Eisenhower died yesterday. Highland Wedding won the Grand National. We went out for dinner to a Chinese (restaurant).'

Apollo 10 launched: 13 May 1969 – 'Apollo 10 went up – good luck! Martha wouldn't come out after tea. I got really mad. Went out with Beth.'

Apollo 10 landed: 26 May 1969 – 'Apollo 10 down safely. Moira, Beth and Barbara gated by AC for talking to James and Oliver outside. Barbara also gated for having her hair out. Listened to *Hair* – it's terrific.'

Sponsored walk for Shelter: 7 June 1969 – 'Set off with Fisherman, accidentally leaving Oliver. We really set a pace, overtaking all the others and my feet began to hurt. We had three cups of tea and didn't stop to eat. Went round all the checkpoints and completed all twenty miles in five hours. Almost everybody got round – they've made tons of money. My feet were all blistered, and I had a huge blood blister. Free cakes at the club. Bathed and went out with Fisherman after tea. I had to be carried.'

Apollo 11 launched: 16 July 1969 – 'Apollo 11 went off today bound to set men on the moon for the first time. I wish them the best of luck and hope they get back safely. In my tiny world, I went shopping in Colwyn Bay, then drove to Rhyl and St Asaph, where we went to see the smallest cathedral in Britain, only to find the Hallé orchestra rehearsing there. It was wonderful to hear them – it was a marvellous sound and all for nothing!'

Apollo 11 moon landing: 21 July 1969 – 'Rose early and watched the first men to walk on the moon live on the telly – is it a beginning or an end? Afraid I can only visualise more wars and hunger because of it. Still, hope they get home safely. Apollo safely off the moon, locked to main bit in space and off for home. Russians evidently crash-landed on the moon. Washed Mum's car – Alex soaked me again and I hit him rather hard. Felt awful about it, I didn't really mean to hit him at all.'

Apollo 12 moon landing: 19 November 1969 – 'Lay in bed listening to the moon landing of Apollo 12. There seems to be a lot wrong with this one, hope they get back okay. The maths exam – oh my God! I only got four done and can only get marks for two of them.'

China/USSR border conflict: 1 October 1969 – 'The Russians and Chinese are at loggerheads again. I'm sure there's going to be a war. Goodbye life for all of us if there is. Rumours right around the school. Tons of prep. My French took me all night and still not finished.'

Miss World Contest: 27 November 1969 – 'Miss Austria won Miss World. Funny the way Nelly calls herself mummy to her dog. Tragic really.'

Rhodesia: 2 March 1970 – 'Rhodesia is a republic. Was first in maths with 63%.'

Eurovision: 21 March 1970 – 'Went down to the rugby, probably the last game I'll see for a long time. We won, naturally, against Kiel. Ireland won the Eurovision Song Contest.'

Grand National: 4 April 1970 – 'Watched TV all night and Gay Trip won the Grand National. Honestly, I'll fail my Highers at this rate. Because I'm at home, I just can't work.'

Apollo 13: 15 April 1970 – 'Apollo 13 is in real trouble in space. Rabble in double maths as usual. Did figure drawing in art and told B I was leaving. The letter doesn't seem to be in yet. I pray it never comes!'

Apollo 13 lands: 17 April 1970 – 'Apollo 13 splashed down safely. Didn't watch it. Worked all night as usual.'

British Aluminium: 17 June 1970 – 'Our British Aluminium trip was cancelled. Workers on strike! Spent all afternoon flower arranging for the junior school fair. Marie and I were picking flowers in Argyll's garden.'

General Election: 18 June 1970 – 'Labour is out. How awful! The Liberals won the school election.'

Bin strike: 31 October 1970 – 'London streets are piled with garbage.'

Ibrox Stadium disaster: 2 January 1971 – 'Twigs phoned, terribly apologetic and upset. We talked for ages, both worried about the people killed at Ibrox today.'

Eurovision: 3 April 1971 – 'Monaco won the Eurovision. Babysat all night across the road – great! On my own all night with plenty to eat. What's more, I get paid.

APPENDIX II

Was this a golden era for film-making? From my diary, here are the films we watched:

1969

The Maggie
A Patch of Blue
The Battle of the Bulge
Lord Jim
Hotel
Fail Safe
Cat Ballou
Wrong Box
If …
The Prime of Miss Jean Brodie
All Quiet on the Western Front
Ring of Bright Water
Star
The File of the Golden Goose
The Graduate
Mackenna's Gold
Oh! What a Lovely War
Carry on Camping

Where Angels Go, Trouble Follows
Hammerhead
Cool Hand Luke
The Bobo
One Million Years B.C.
The Battle of Britain
The Bank Breaker
A Man for All Seasons
Not with My Wife You Don't
One Hundred and One Dalmatians
Suicide Mission
First Men in the Moon
Romeo and Juliet
Goodbye, Mr Chips
The Virgin Soldiers
The Long Ships
You Must Be Joking!

1970

Bullitt
Bonnie and Clyde
The Inn of the Sixth Happiness
The Prize
Breakfast at Tiffany's
Hello Dolly!
The Yellow Rolls Royce
The Four Horsemen of the Apocalypse
Midnight Cowboy
On Her Majesty's Secret Service
Boy on a Dolphin

Where Eagles Dare
Butch Cassidy and the Sundance Kid
John and Mary
Ann of the Thousand Days
The Magic Christian
Entertaining Mr Sloane
Poor Cow
Alice's Restaurant
Hoffman
The Man Who Haunted Himself
Alice in Wonderland
Grand Prix
Airport
Woodstock
The African Queen
A Man Called Horse
The Treasure of Sierra Madre
The Magnificent Seven
The Virgin and the Gypsy
Fahrenheit 451
Kind Hearts and Coronets
Sweet Charity
Kelly's Heroes
Arsenic and Old Lace
Bob and Carol and Ted and Alice
The Thomas Crown Affair
Zabriskie Point
2001: A Space Odyssey
Cry, the Beloved Country
Oliver

1971

The Green Berets
Carmen Jones
Around the World in Eighty Days
Hannibal Brooks
Otley
Dr Dolittle
Ryan's Daughter
On the Beach
David Copperfield
The Aristocats
Start the Revolution Without Me
The Prime of Miss Jean Brodie
The Apartment
Tom Jones
Che
Little Big Man
The Italian Job
Zeppelin
Love Story
Get Carter
Villain
The Go-Between
What did you do in the War, Daddy?
The Dirty Dozen
Soldier Blue
MASH

Printed in Great Britain
by Amazon

60825643R00150